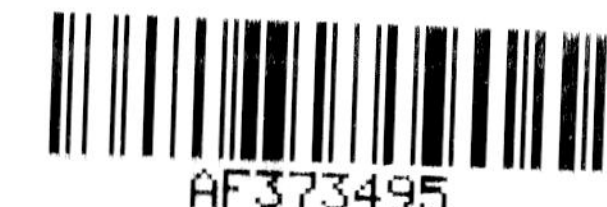

THIS COLORING BOOK
BELONGS TO :

____

- -

____

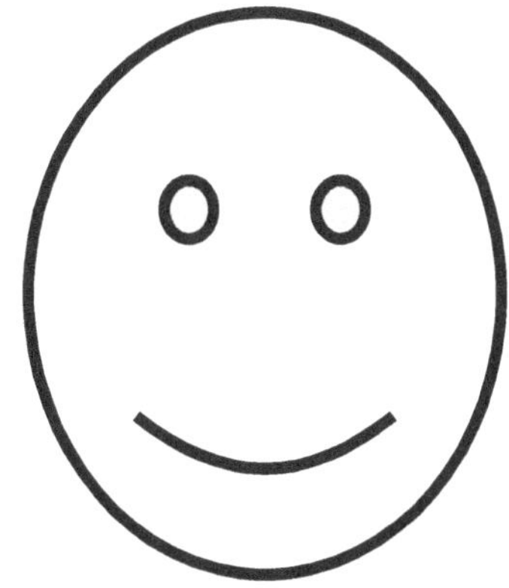

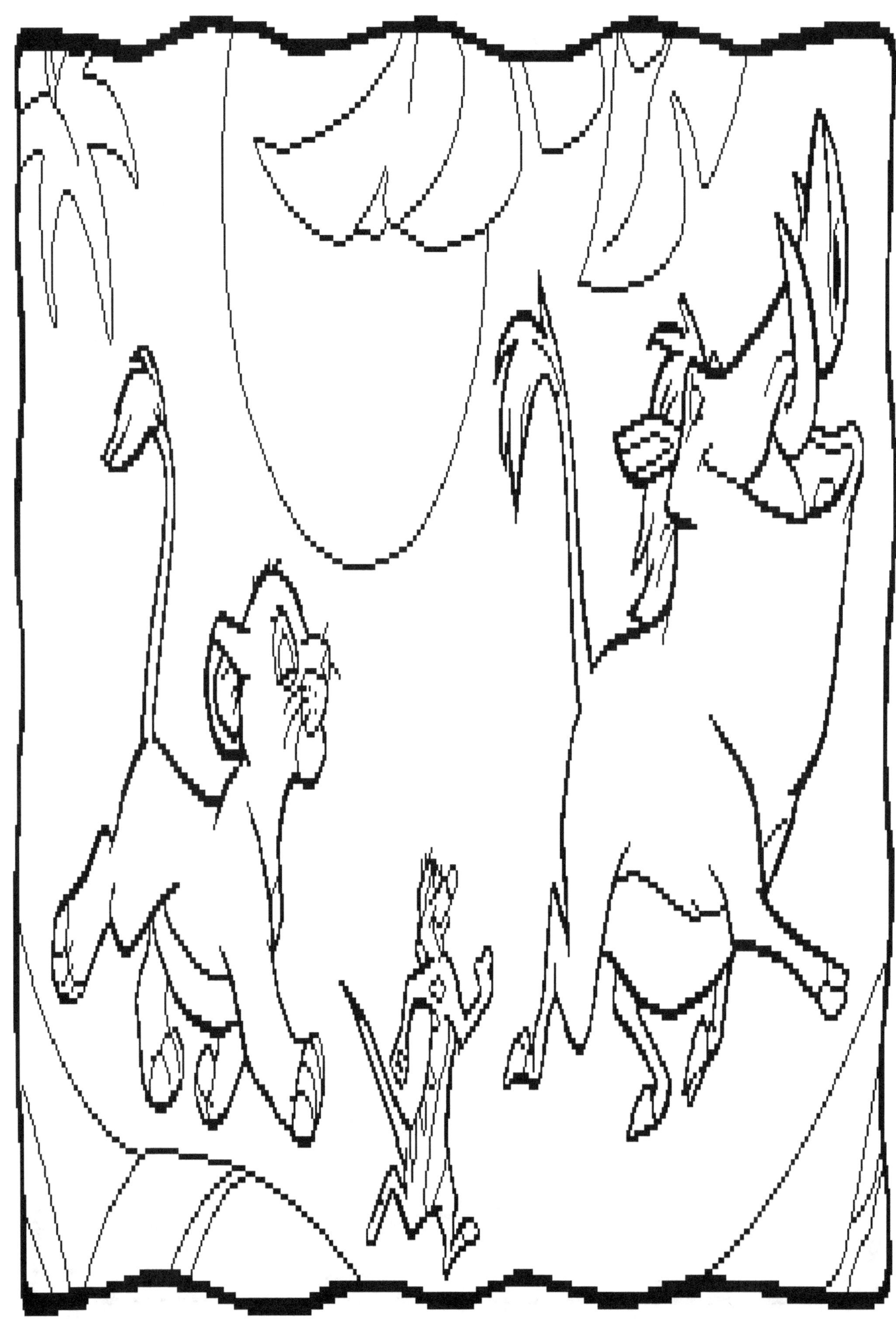

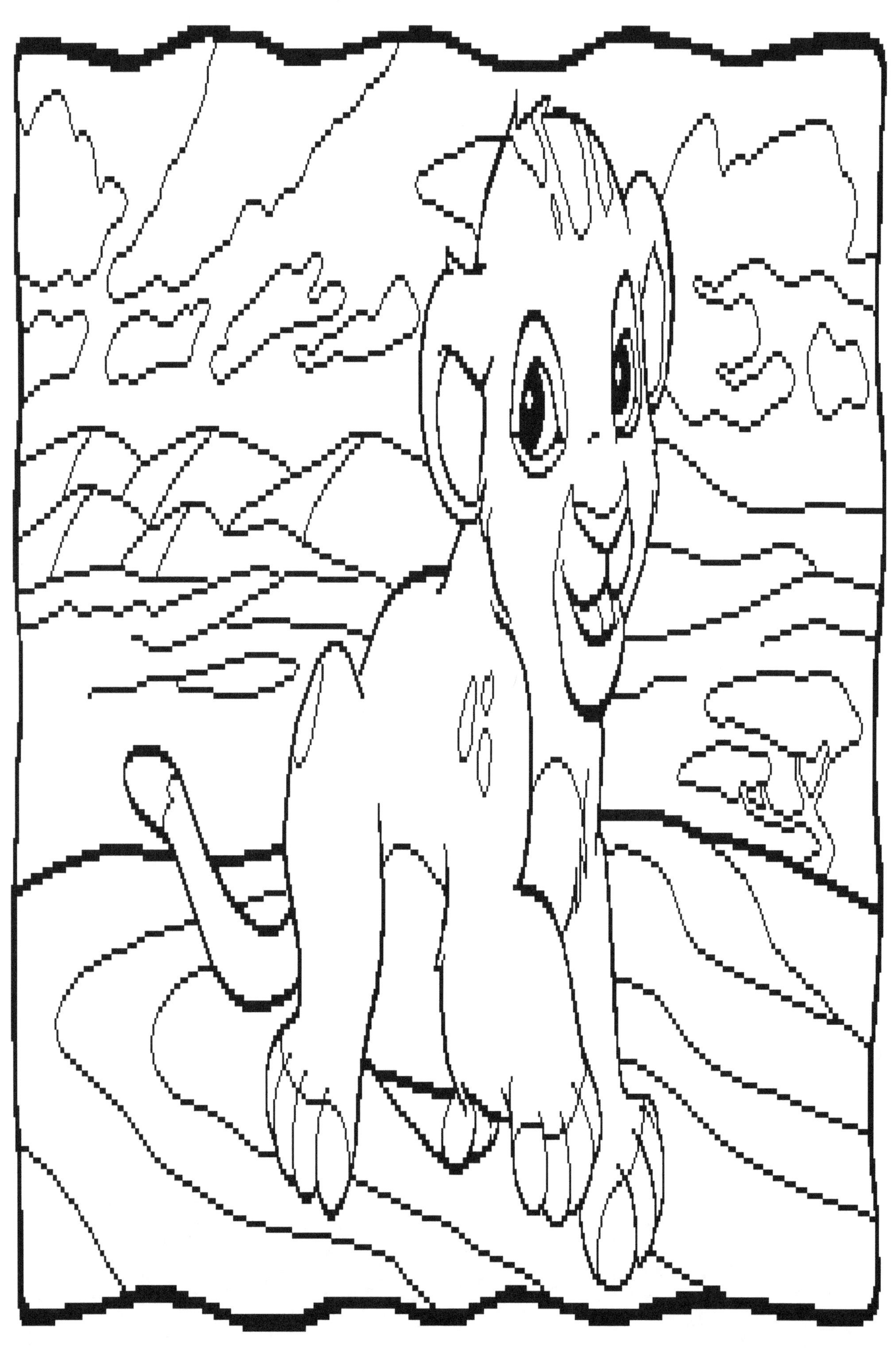

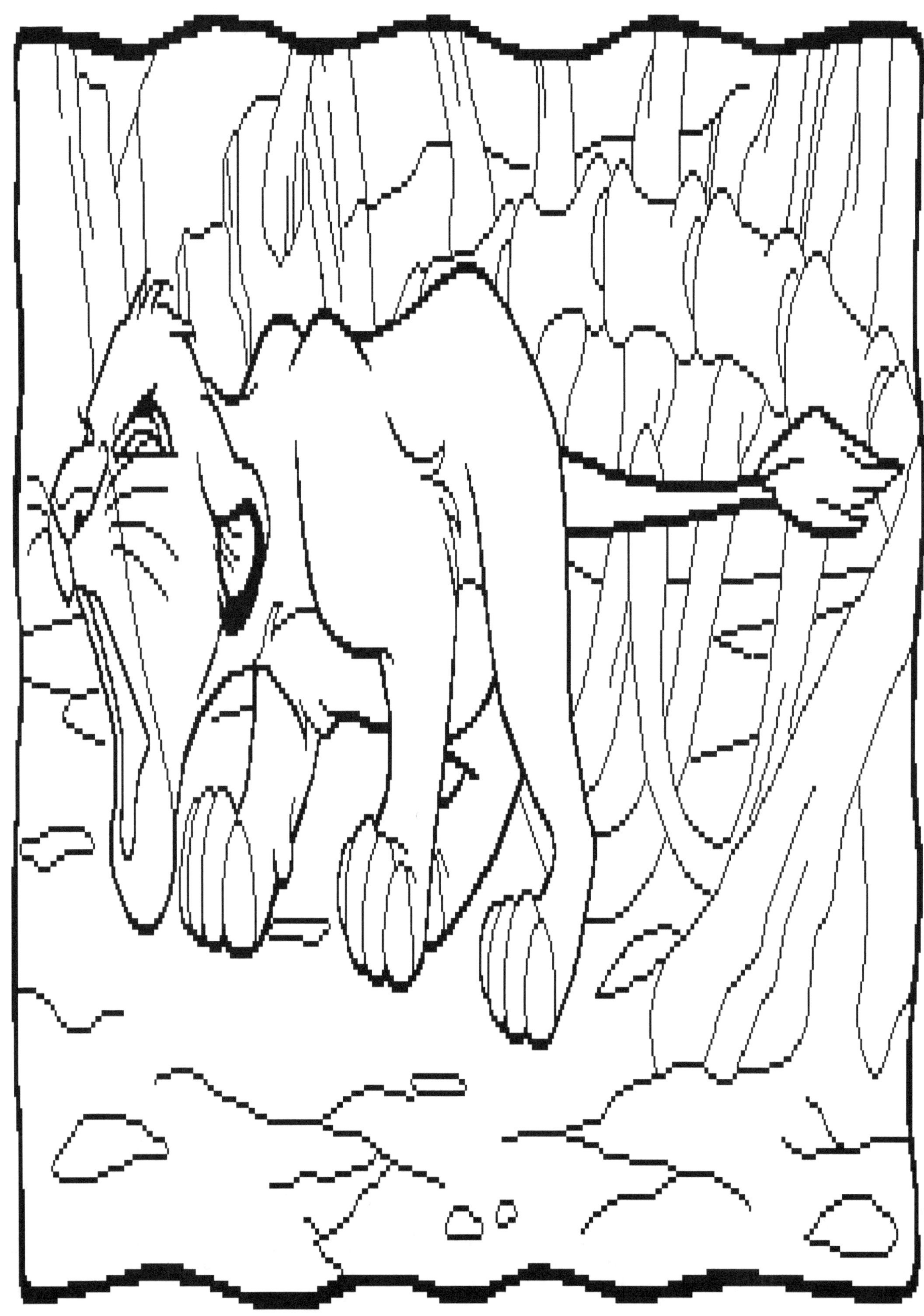

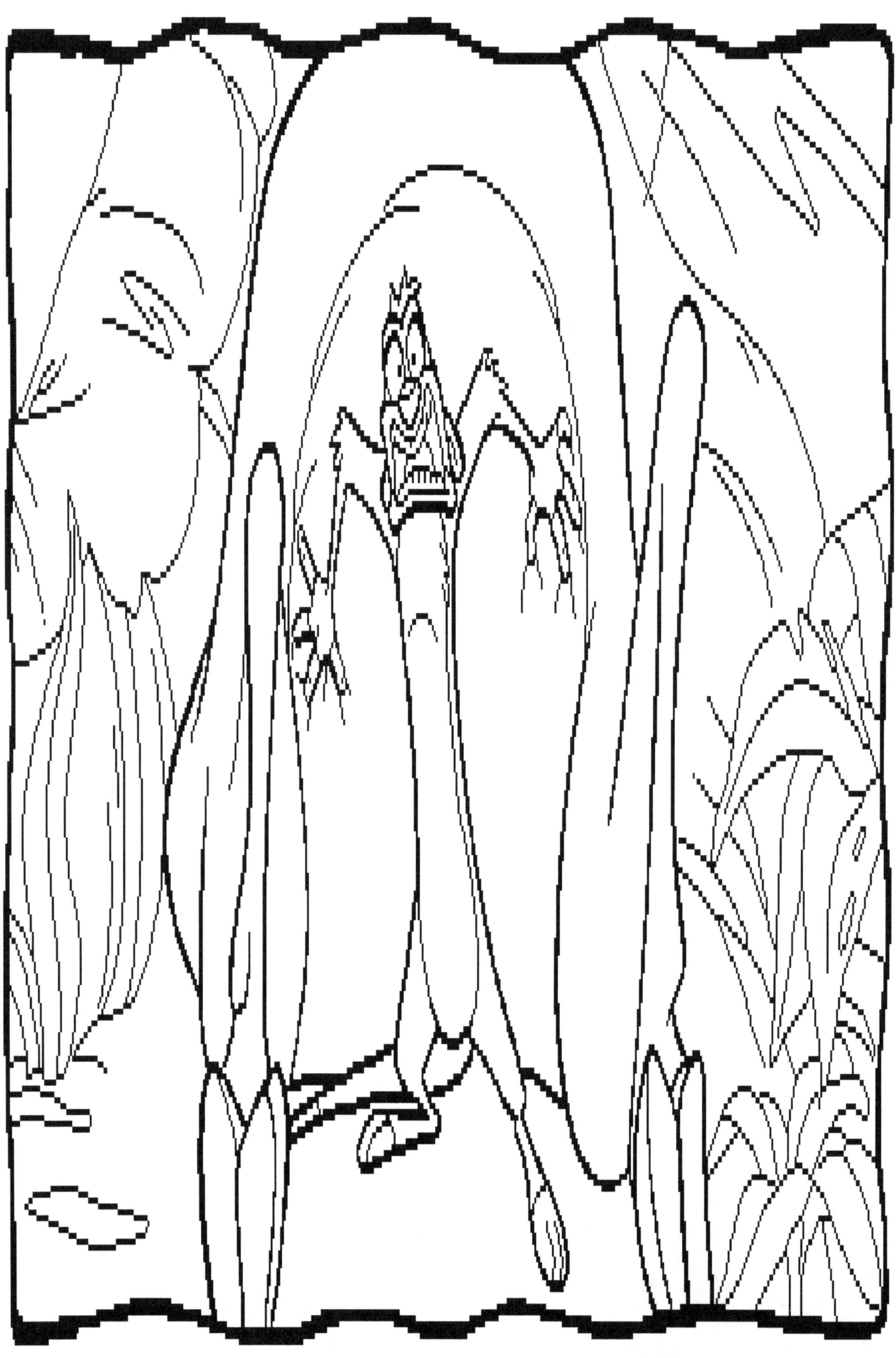

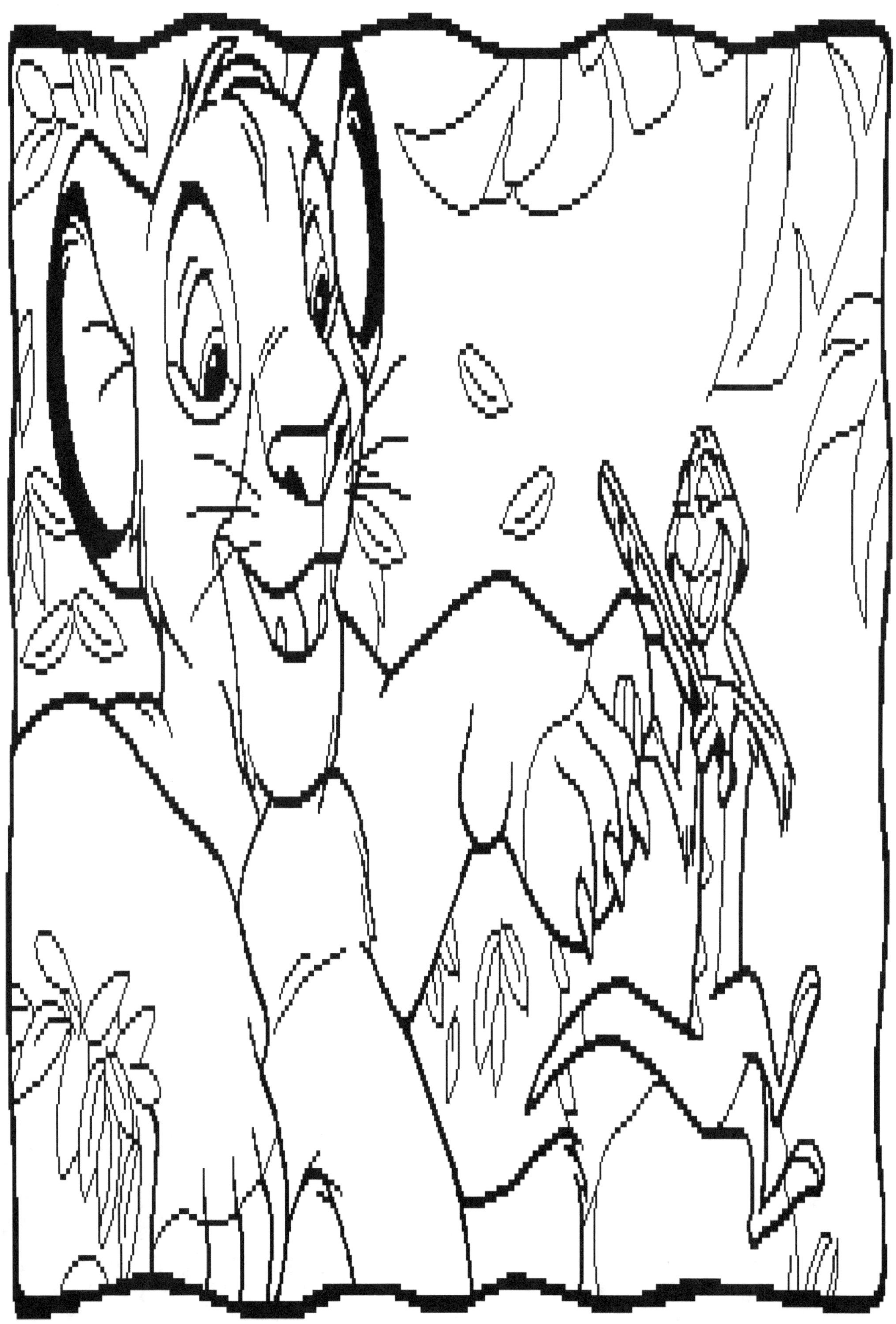

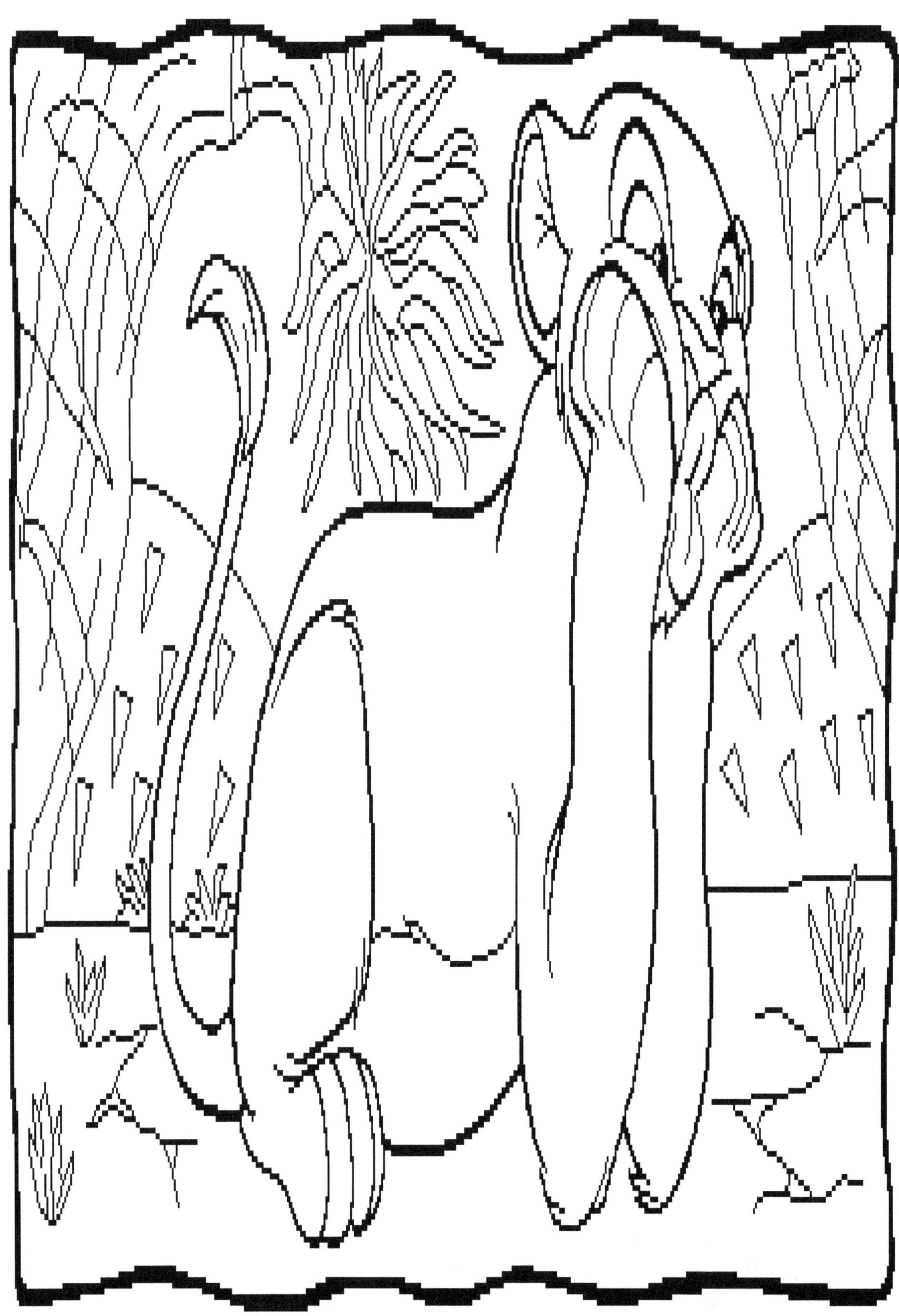

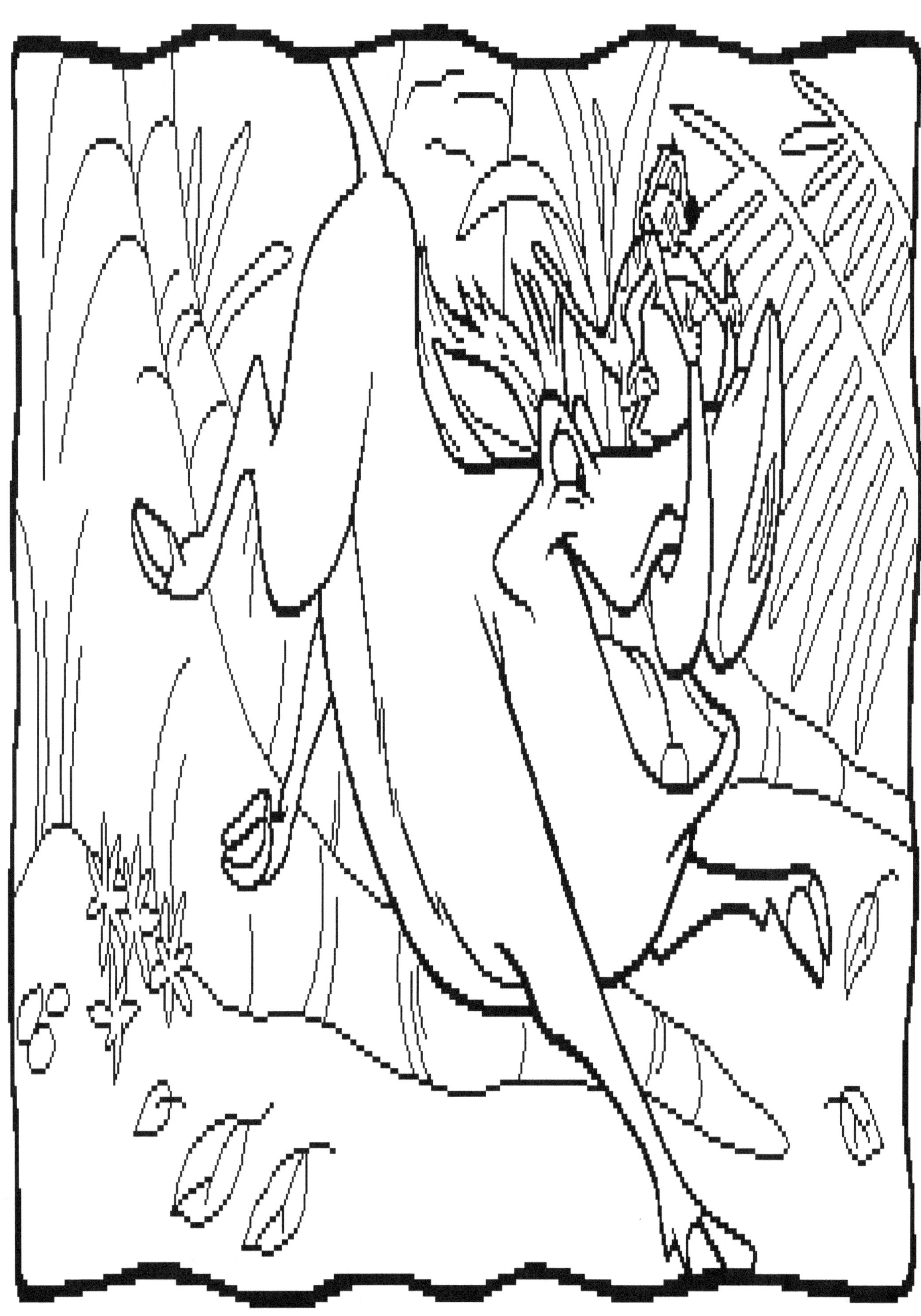

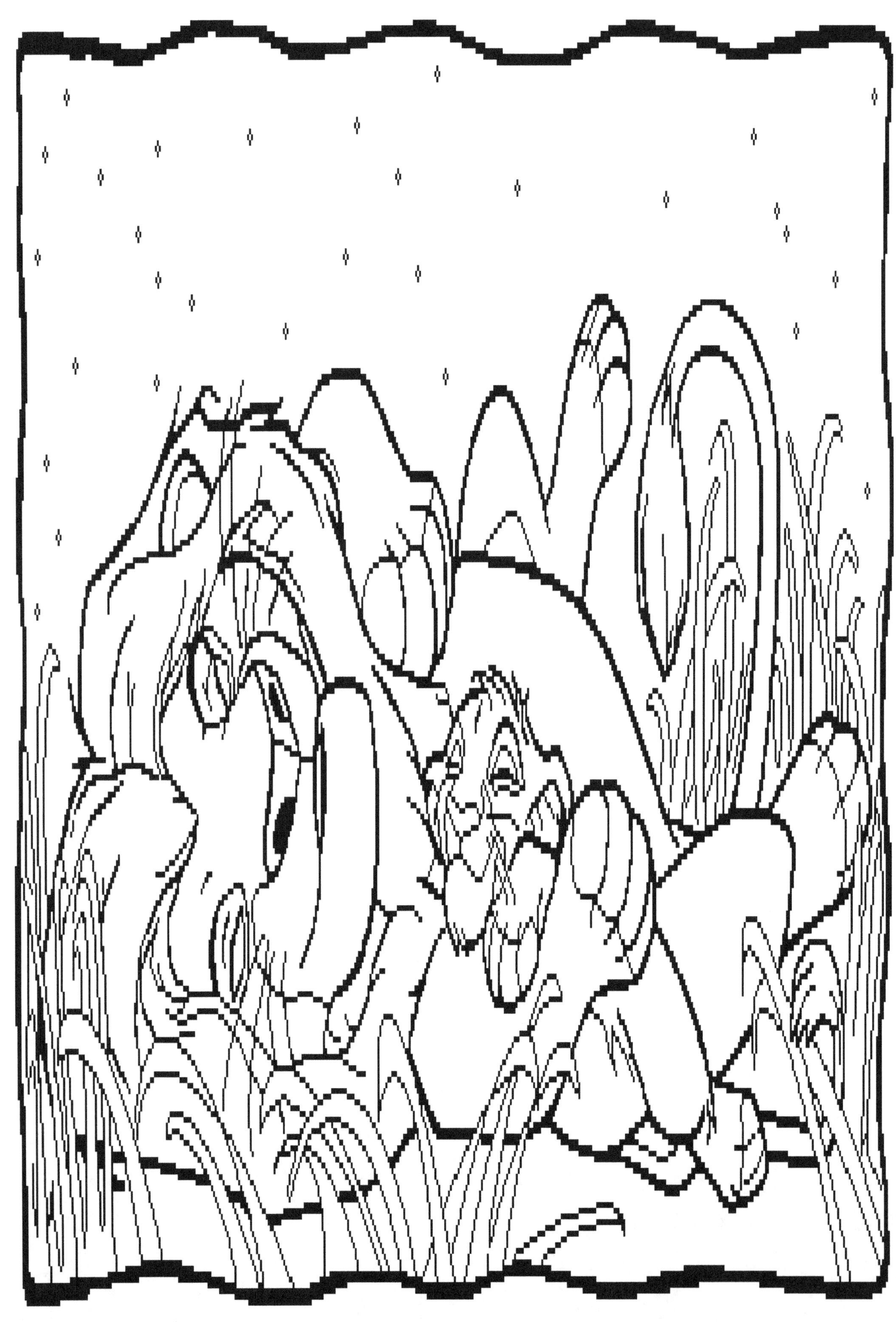

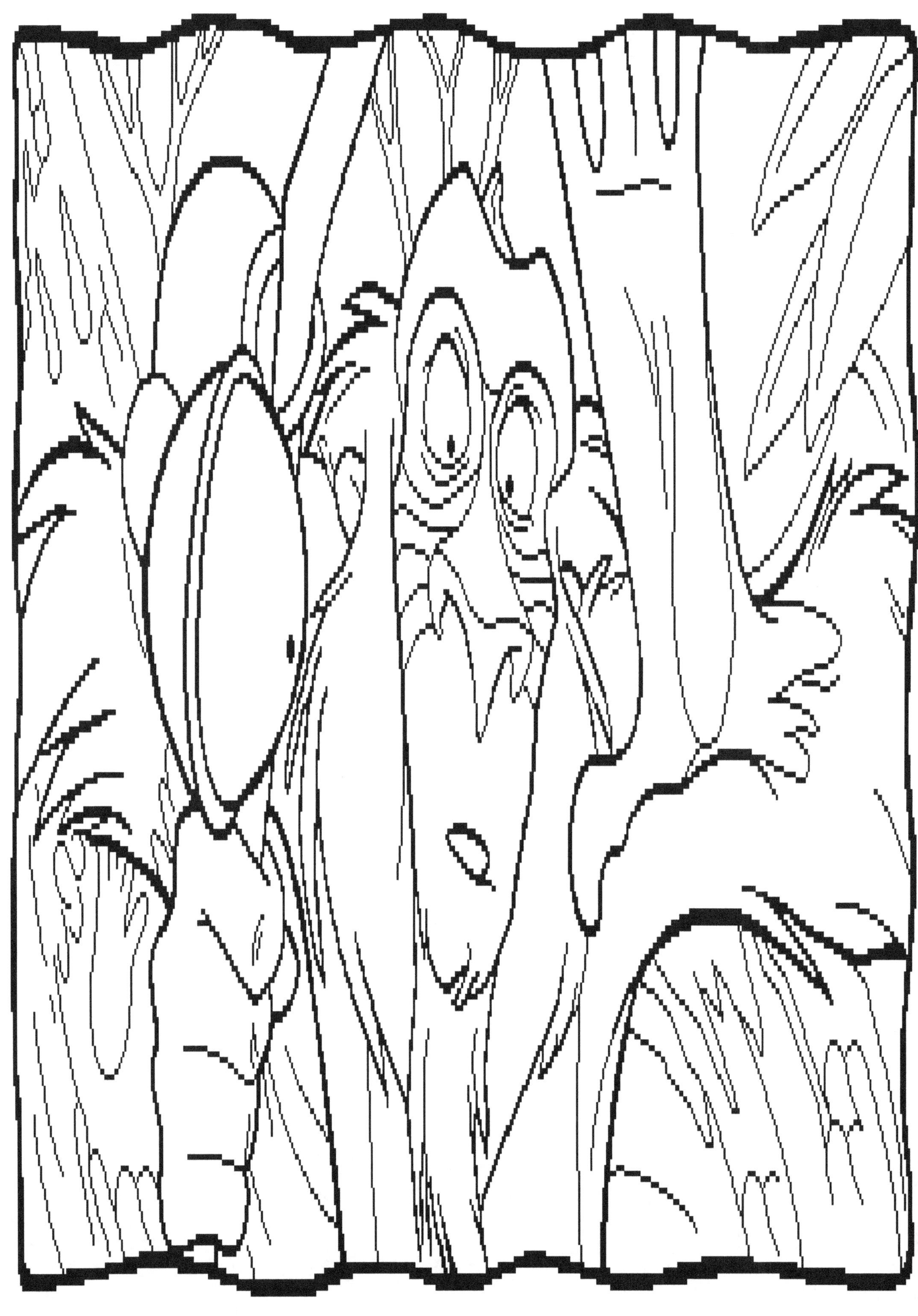

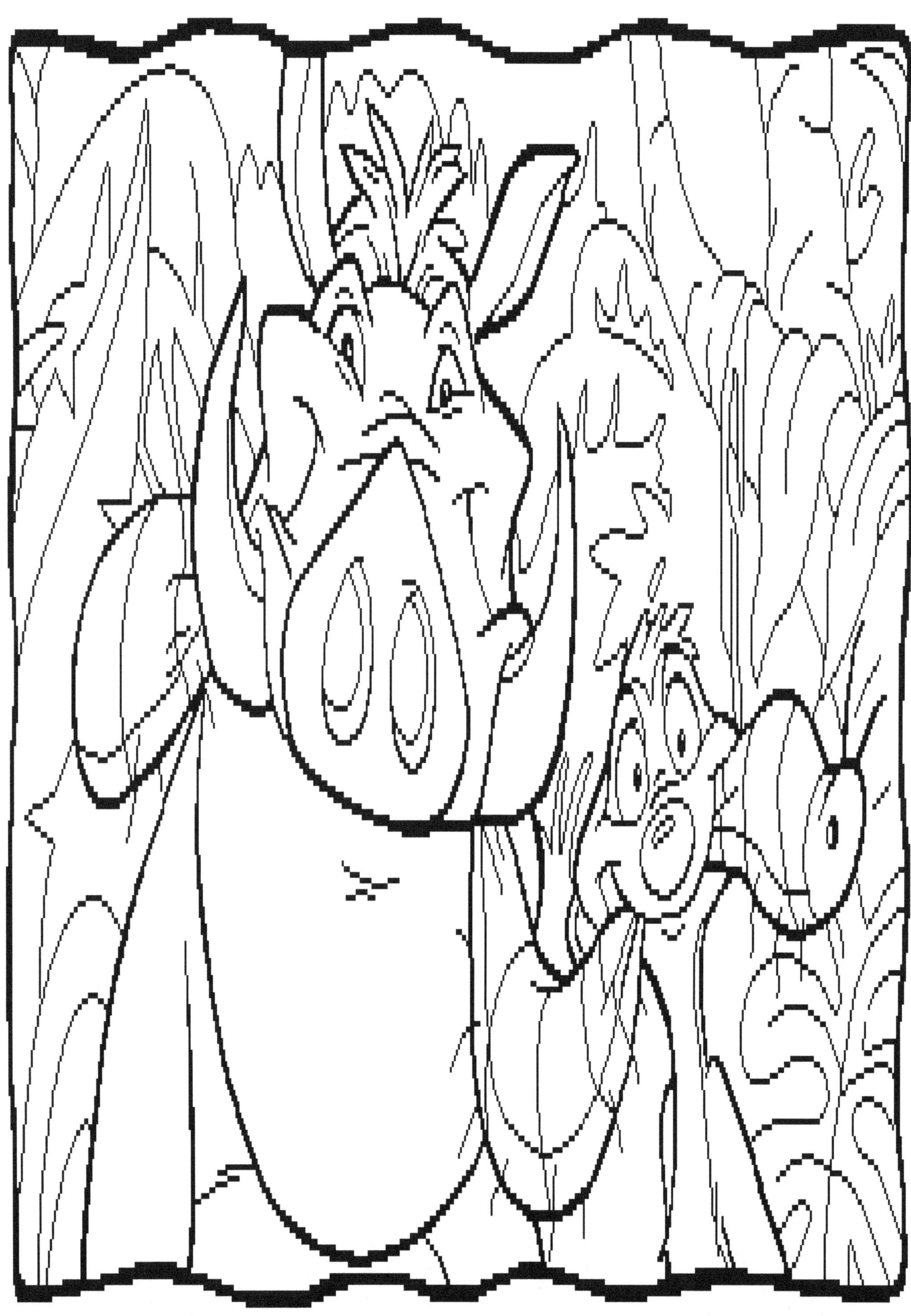

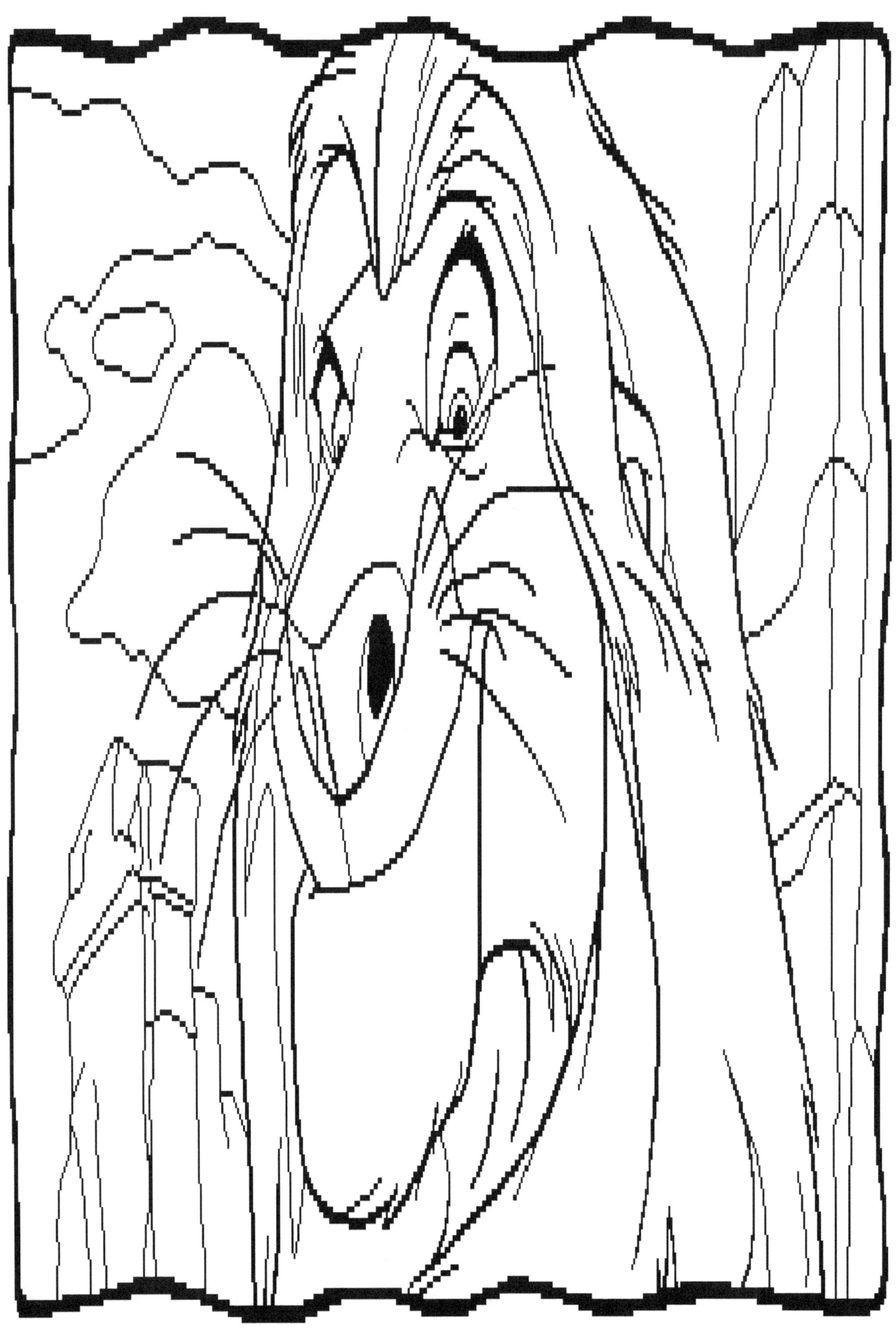

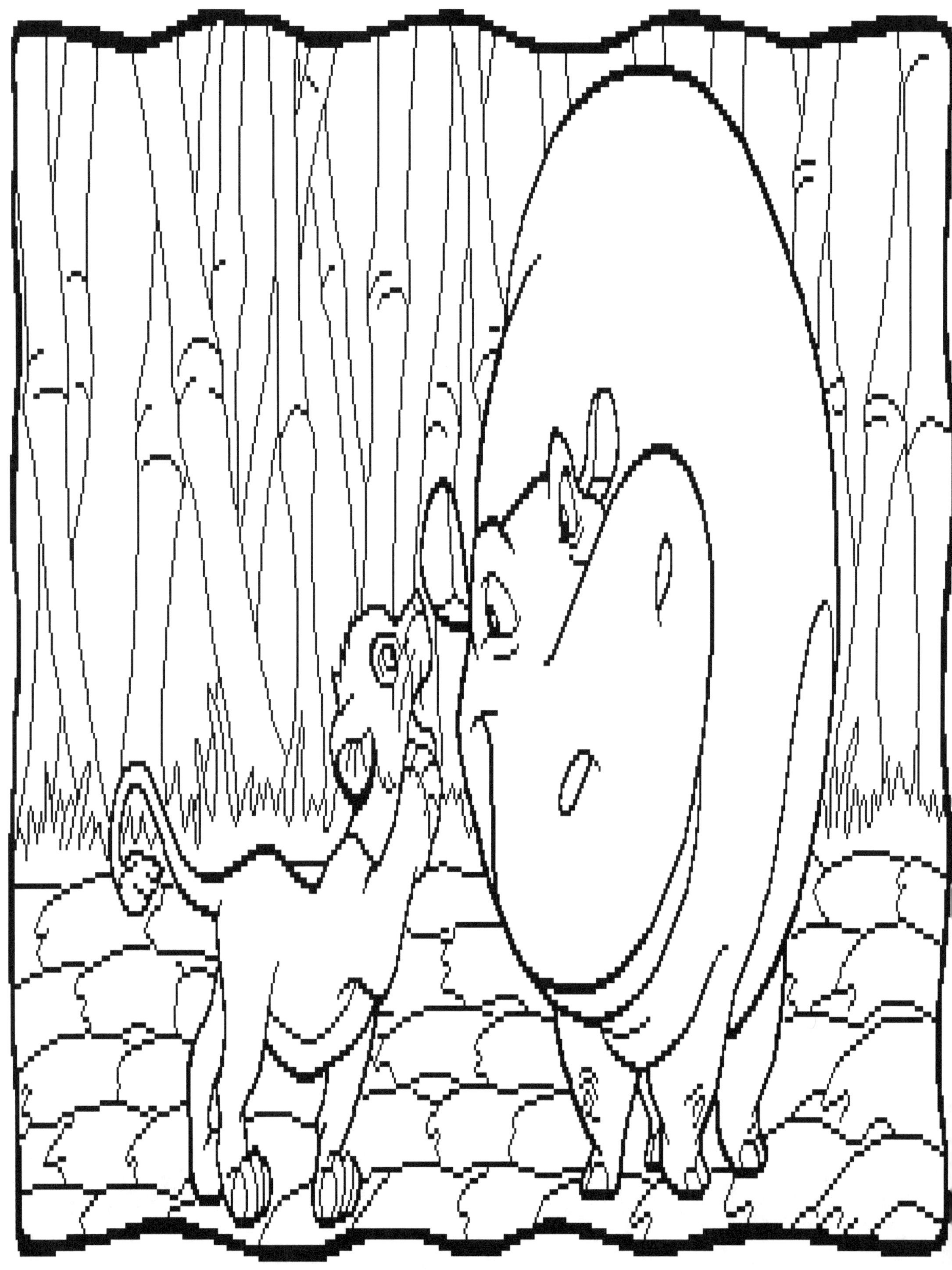

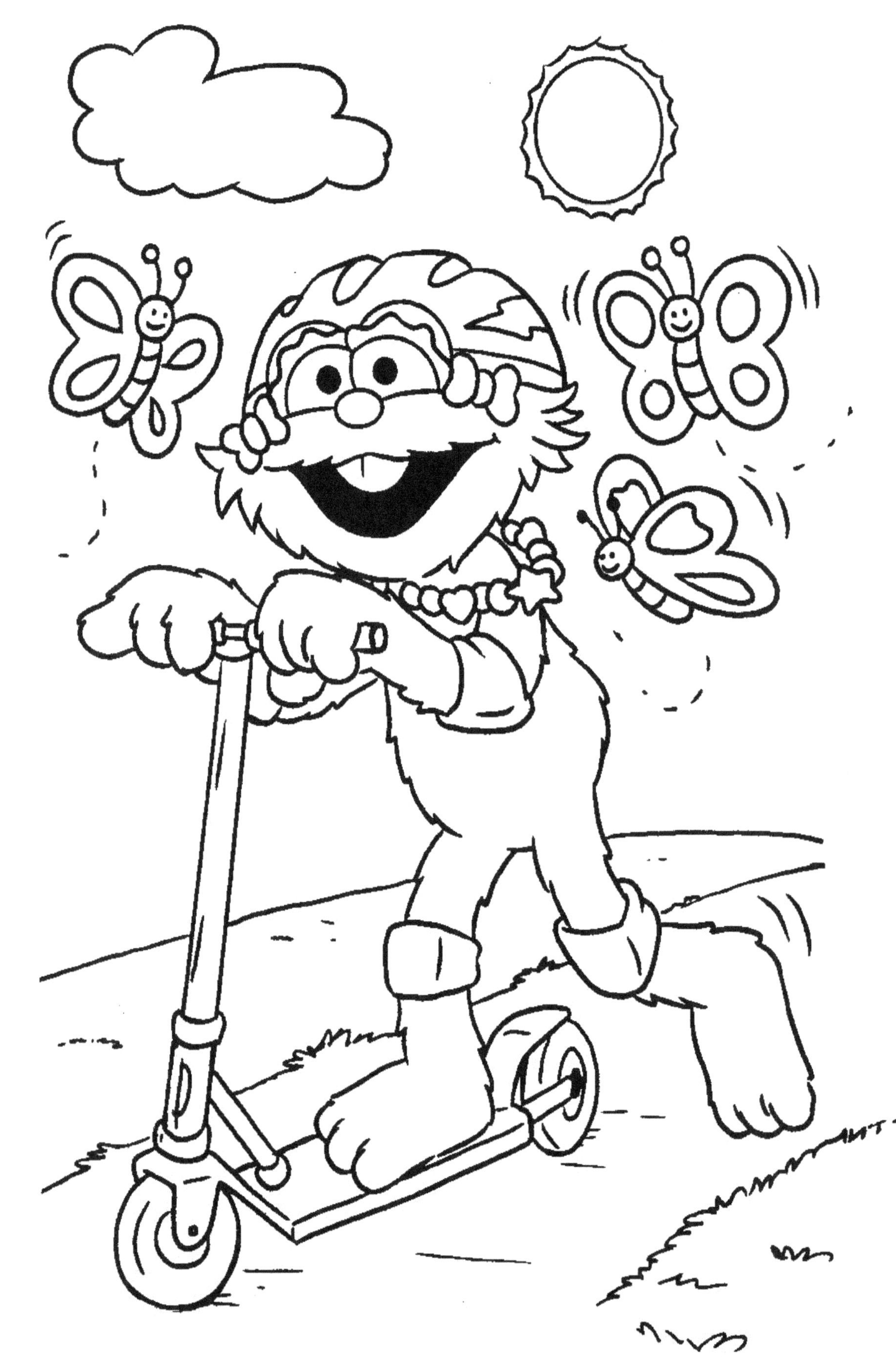

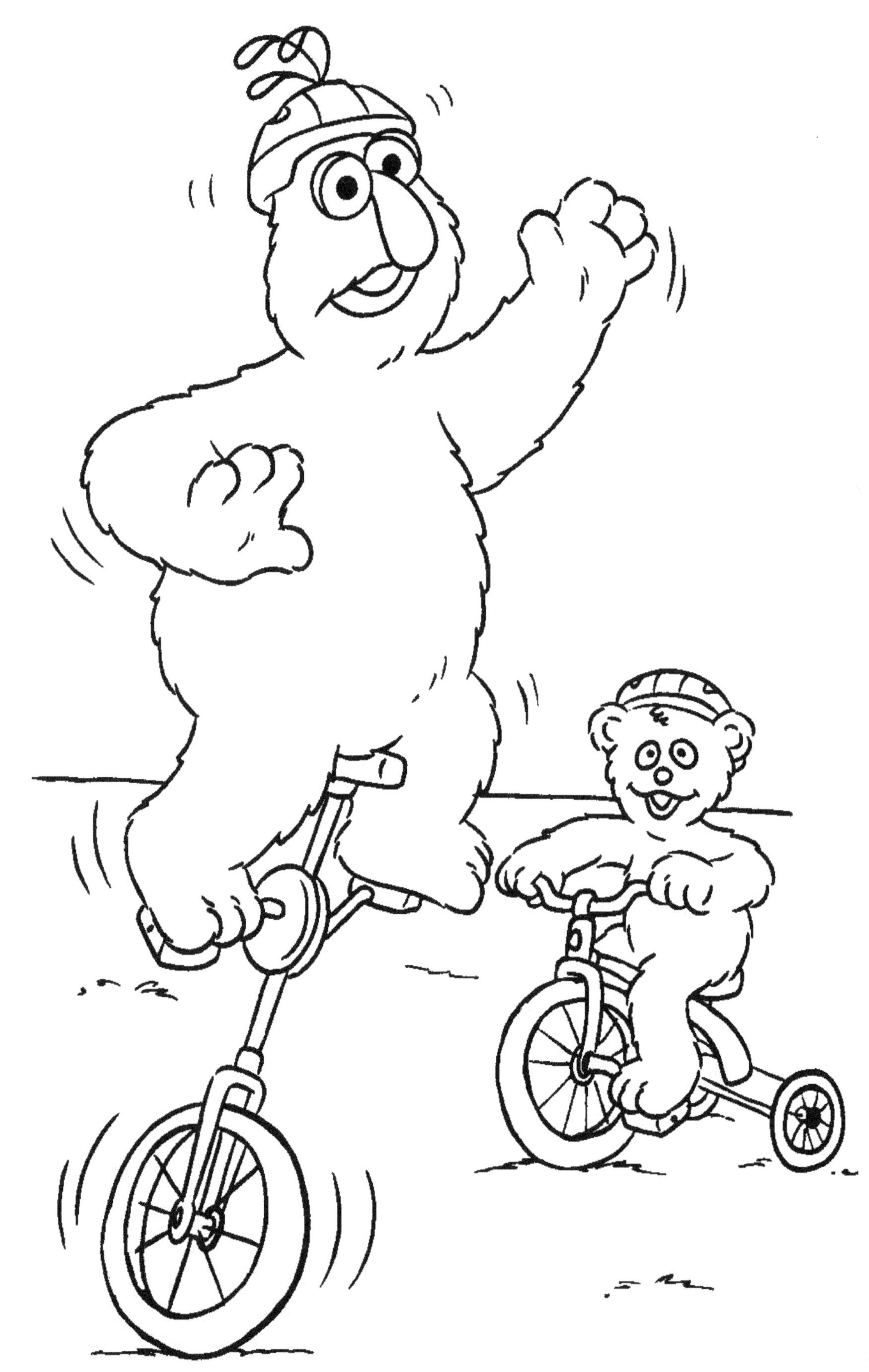

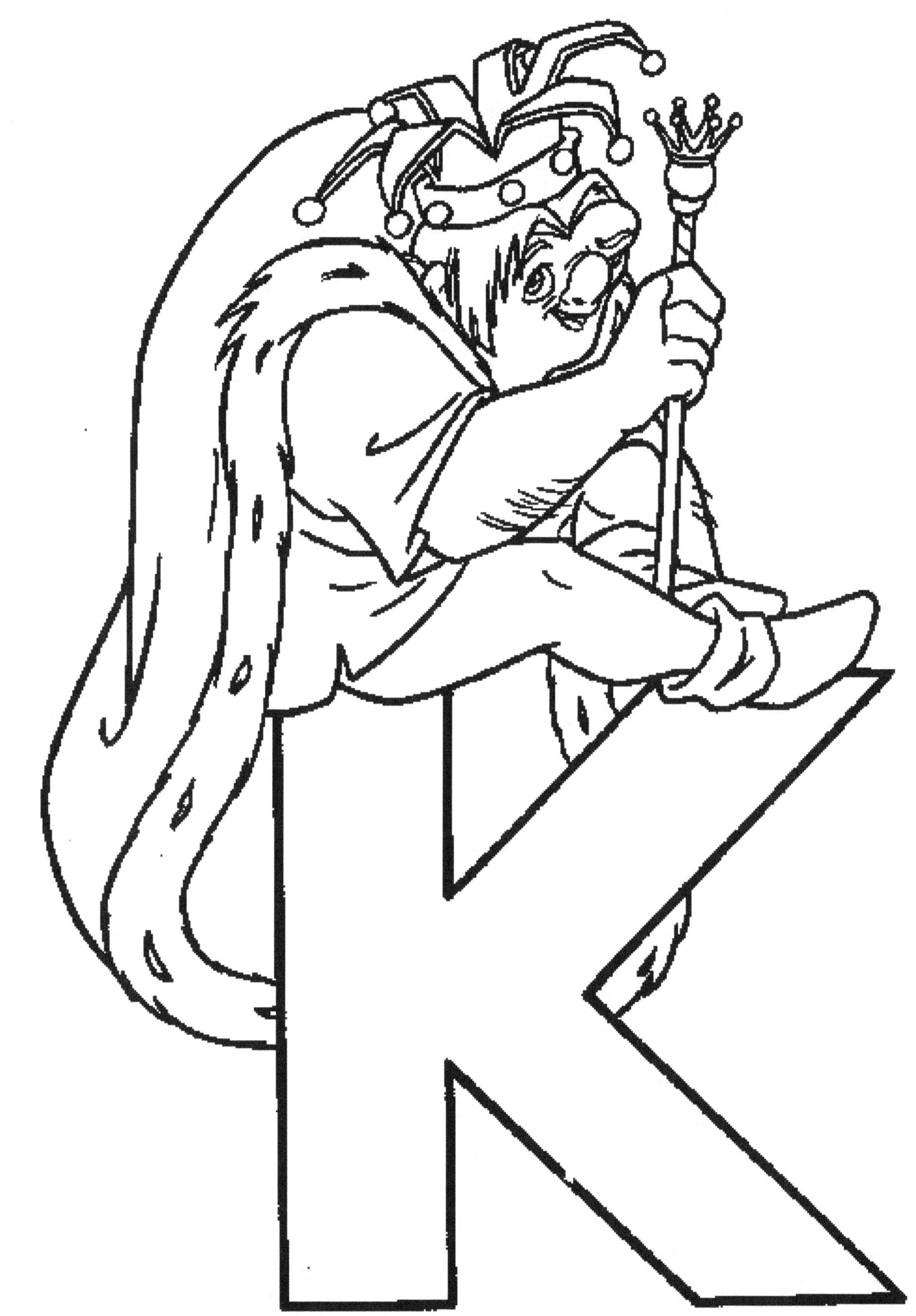

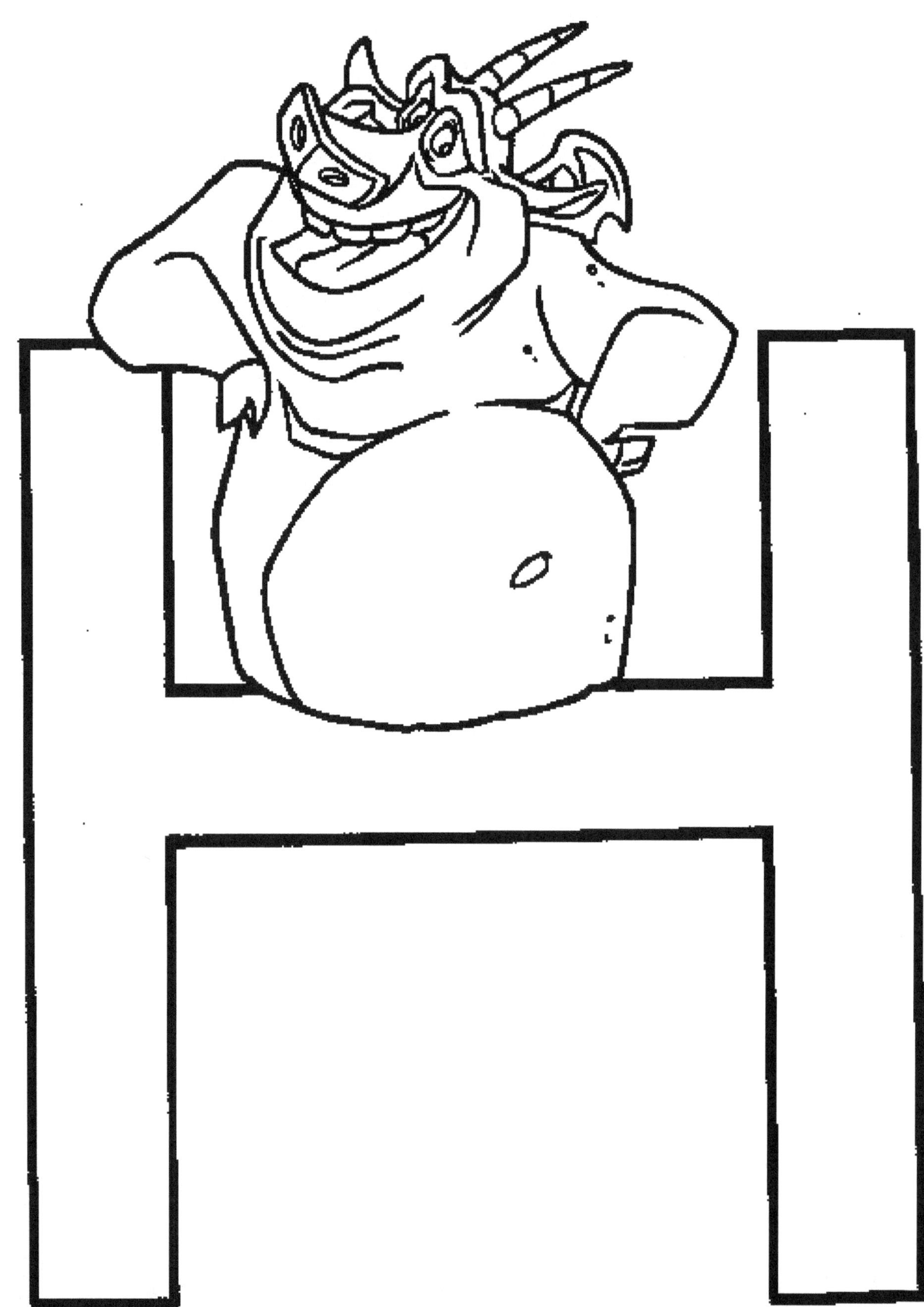

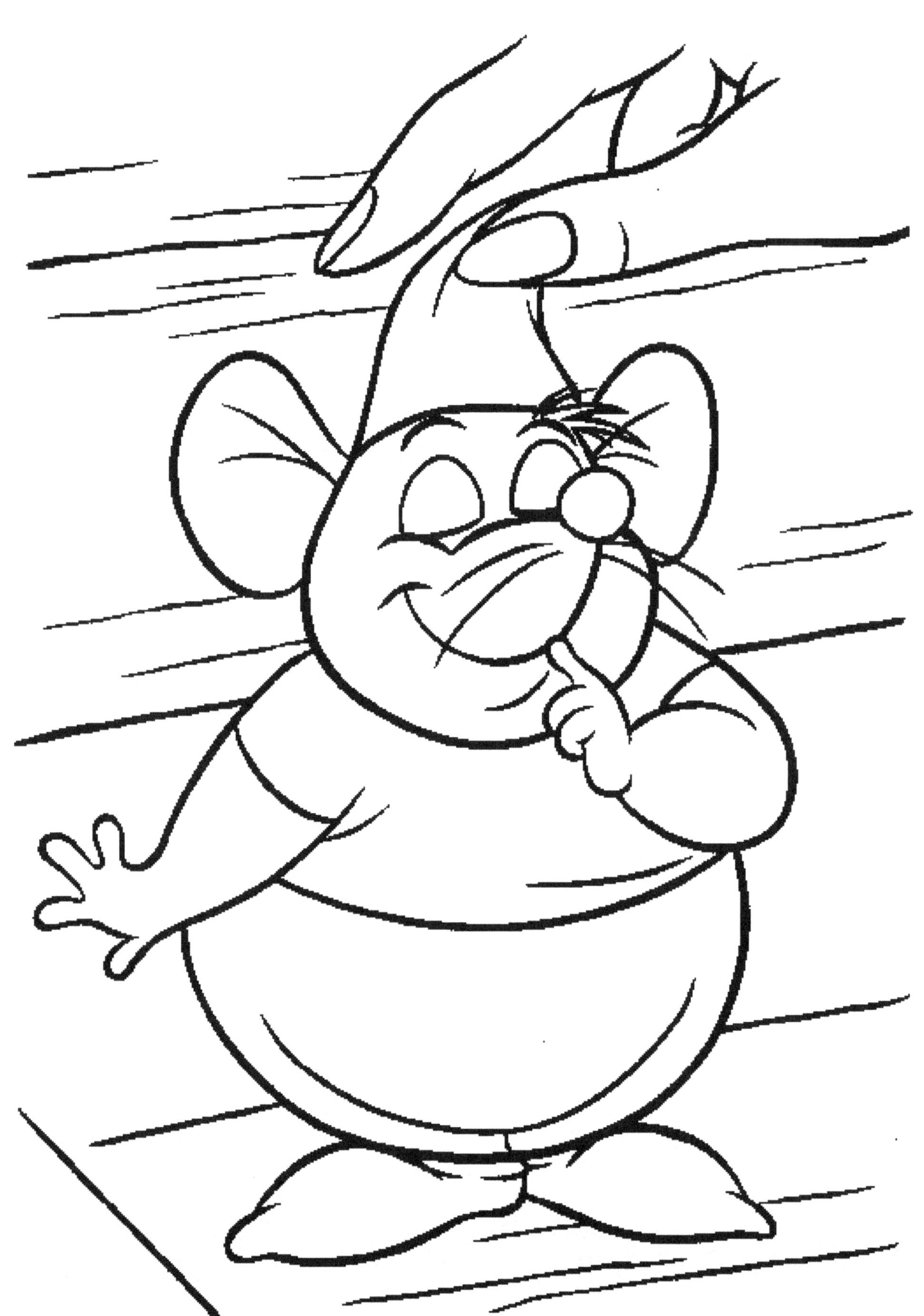

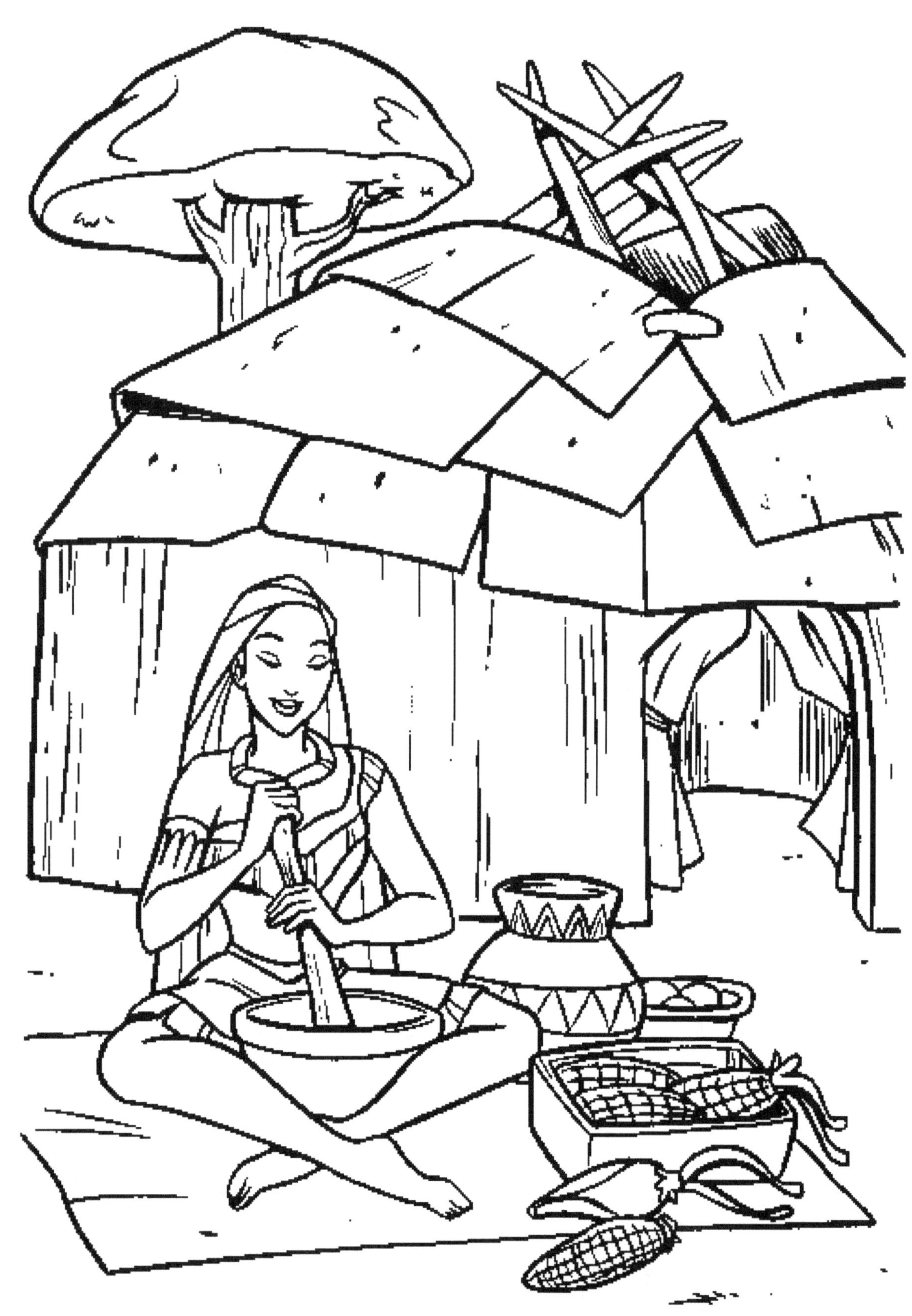

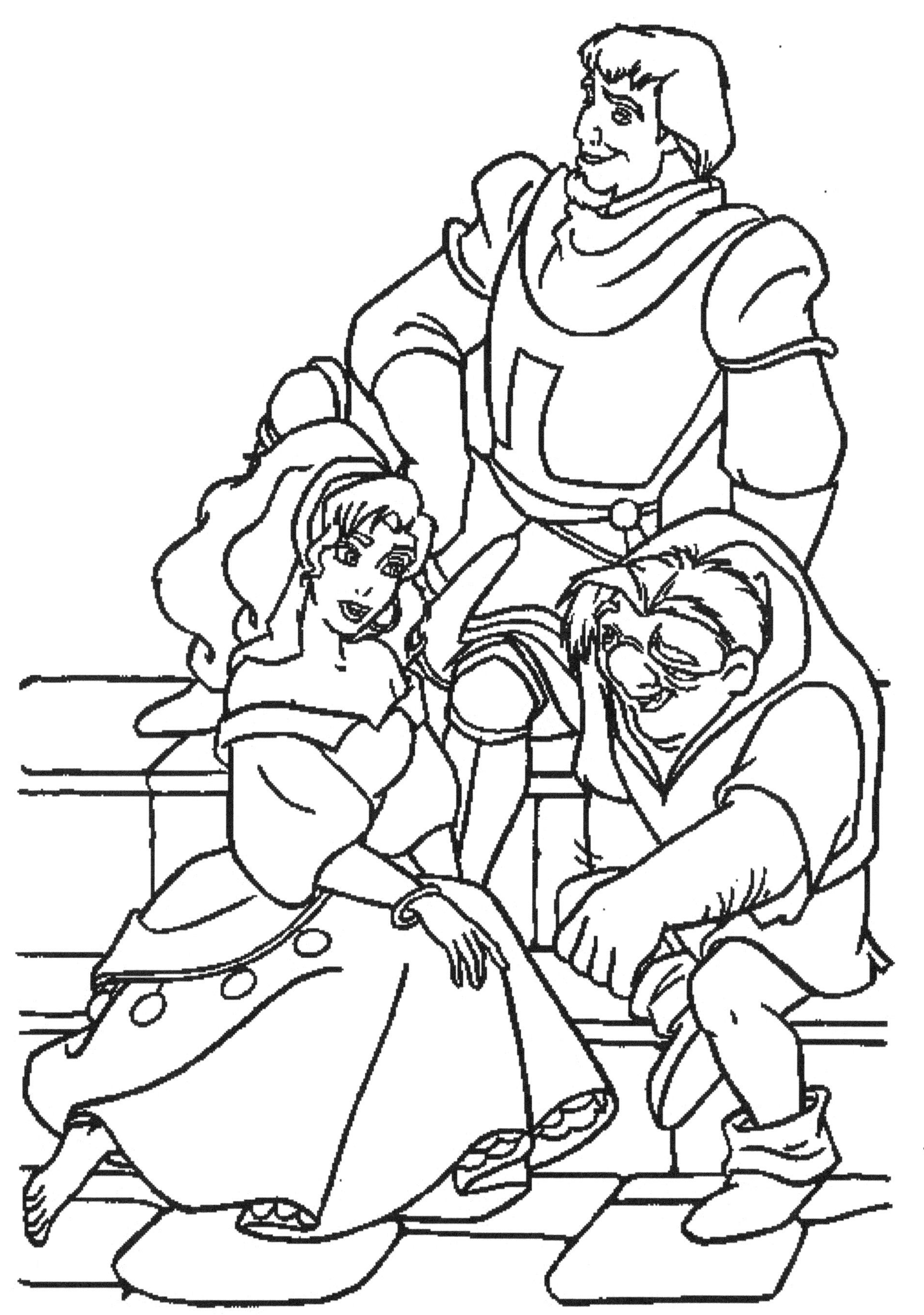

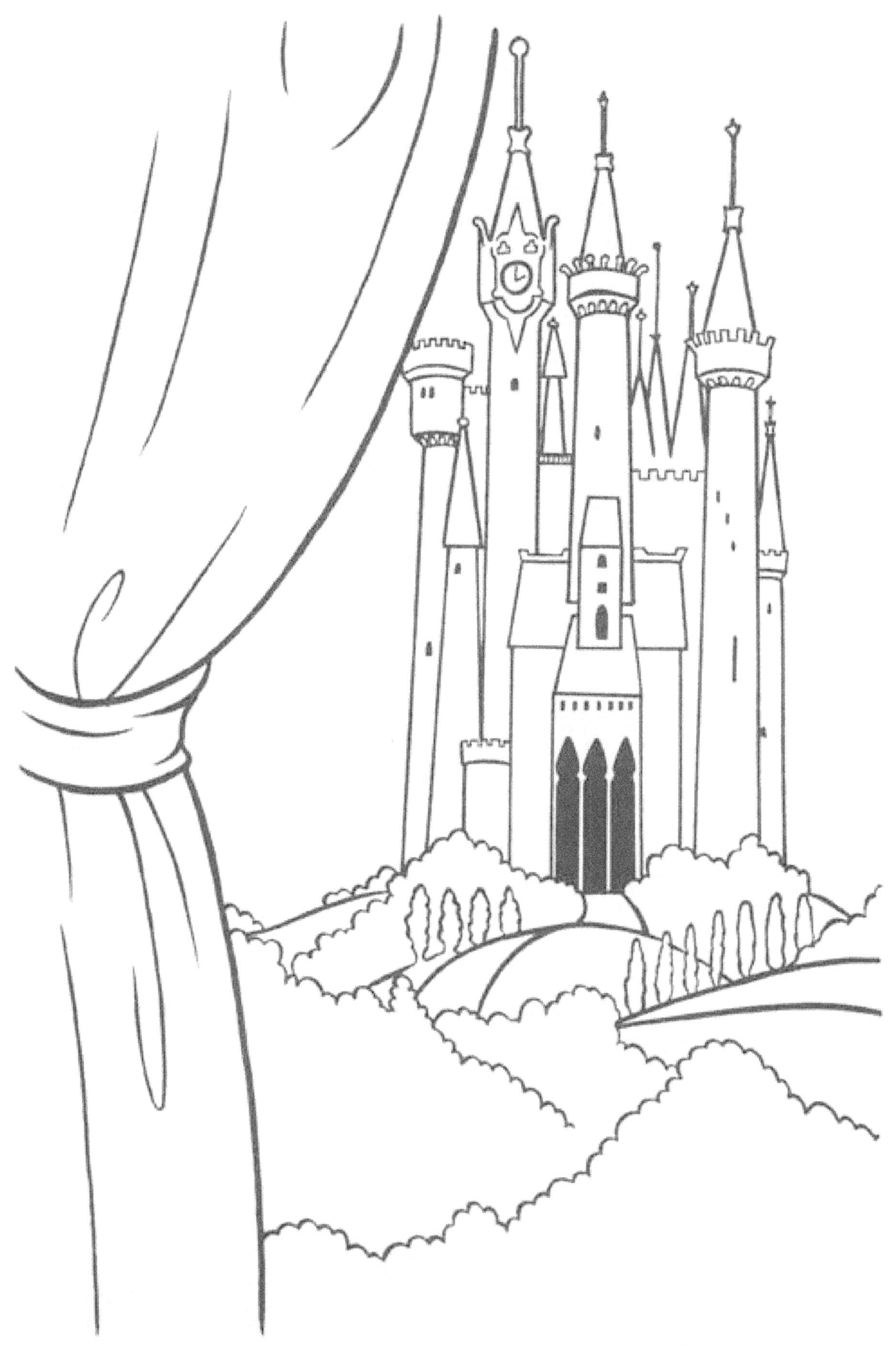

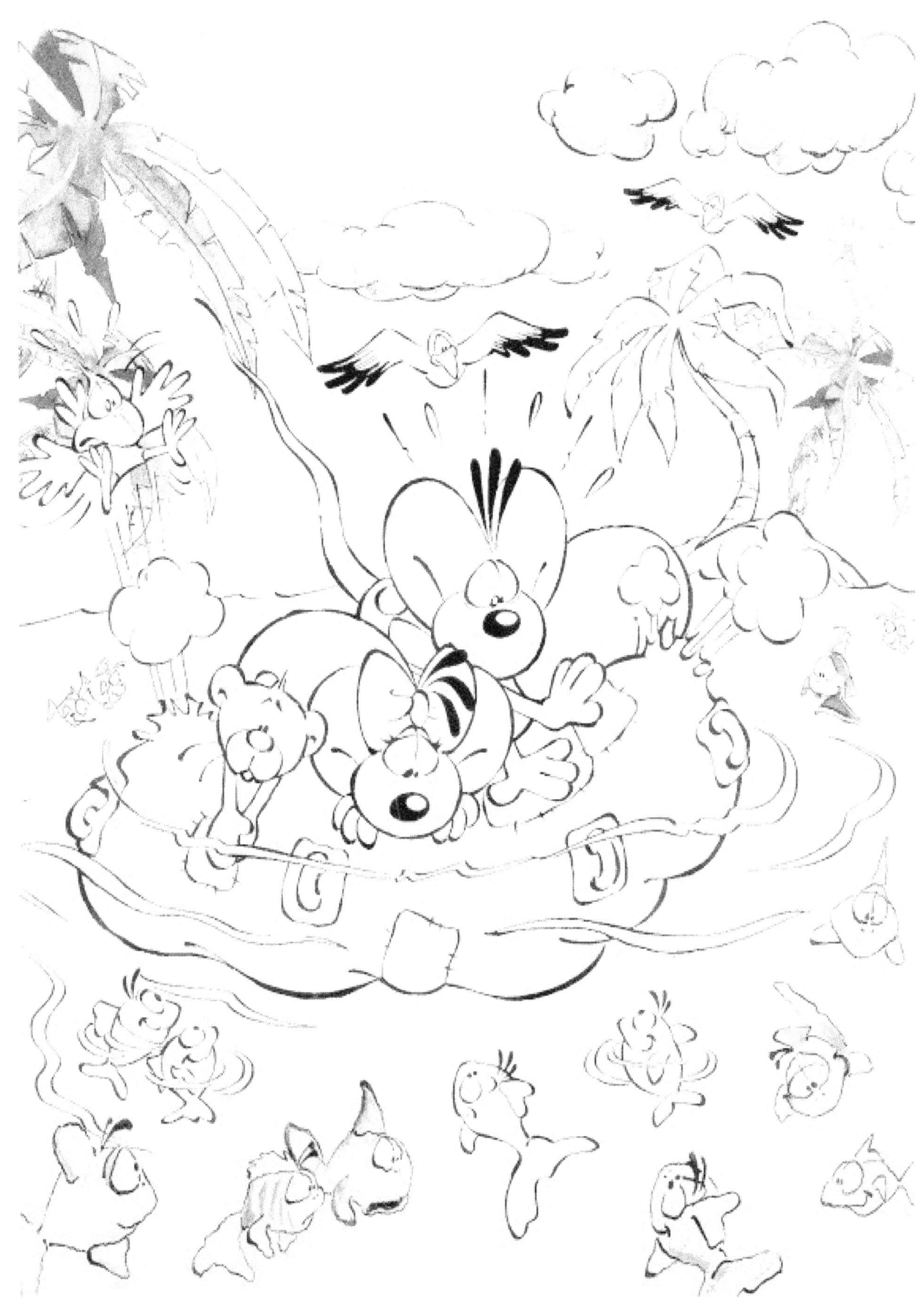

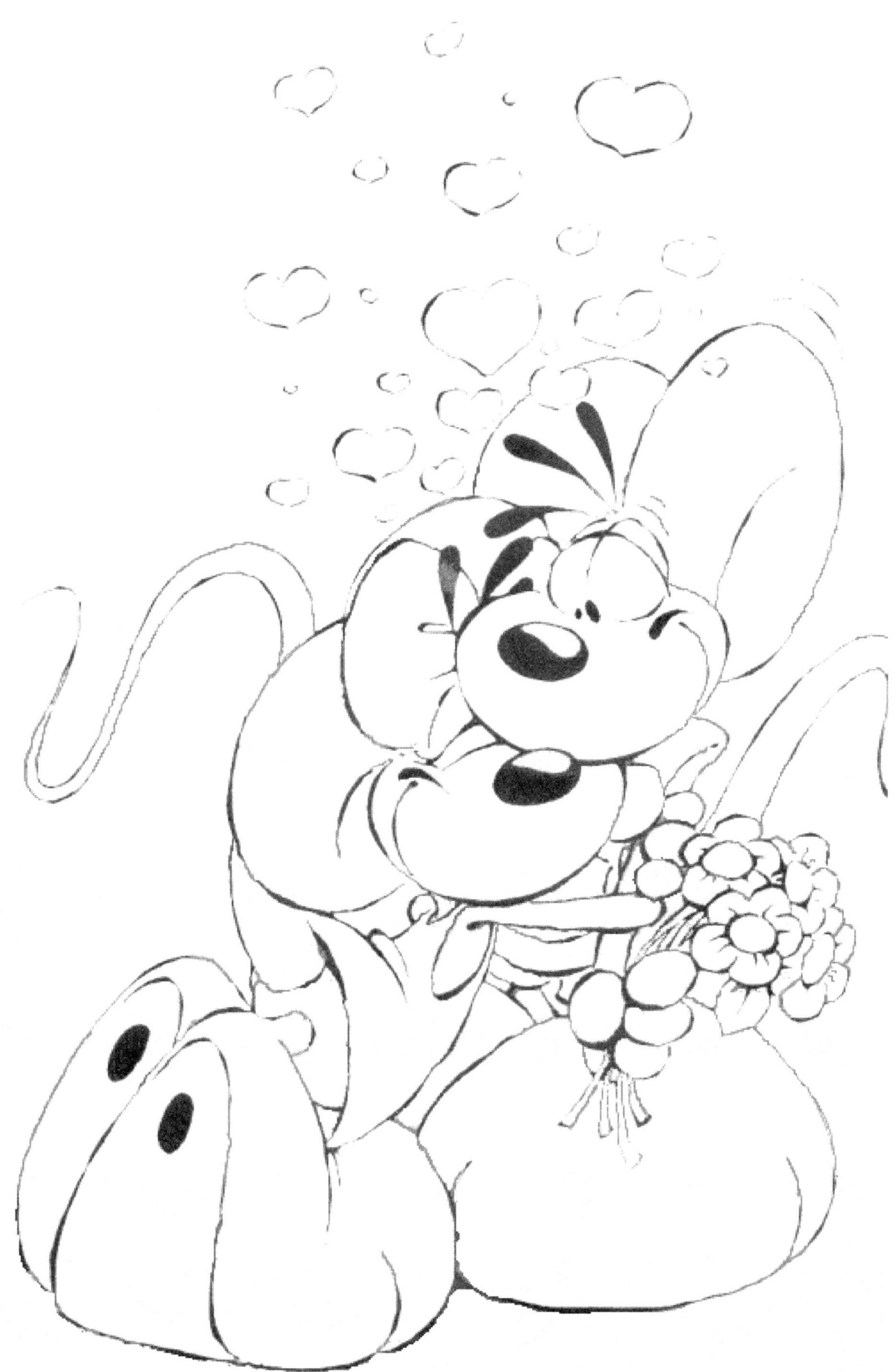

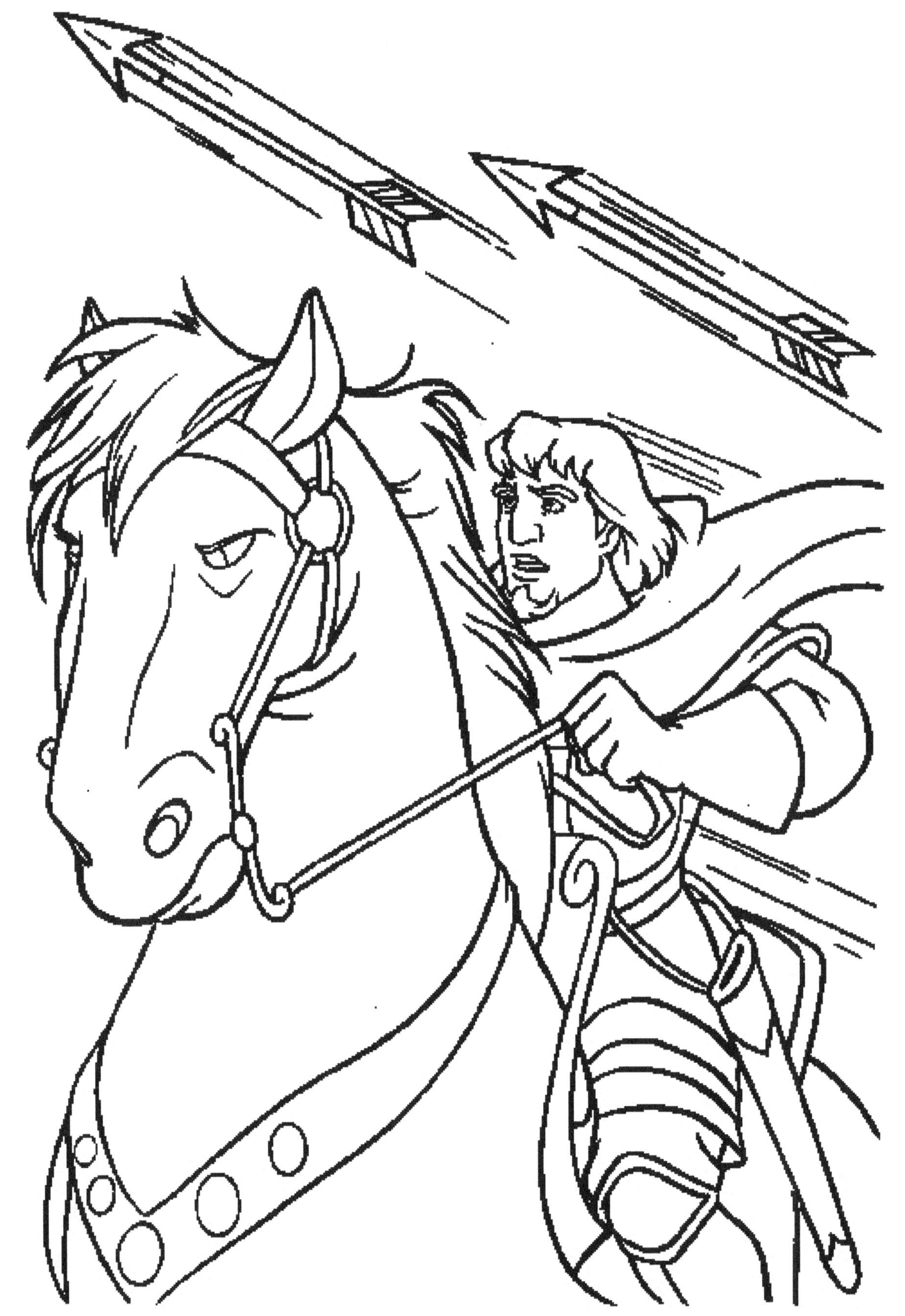

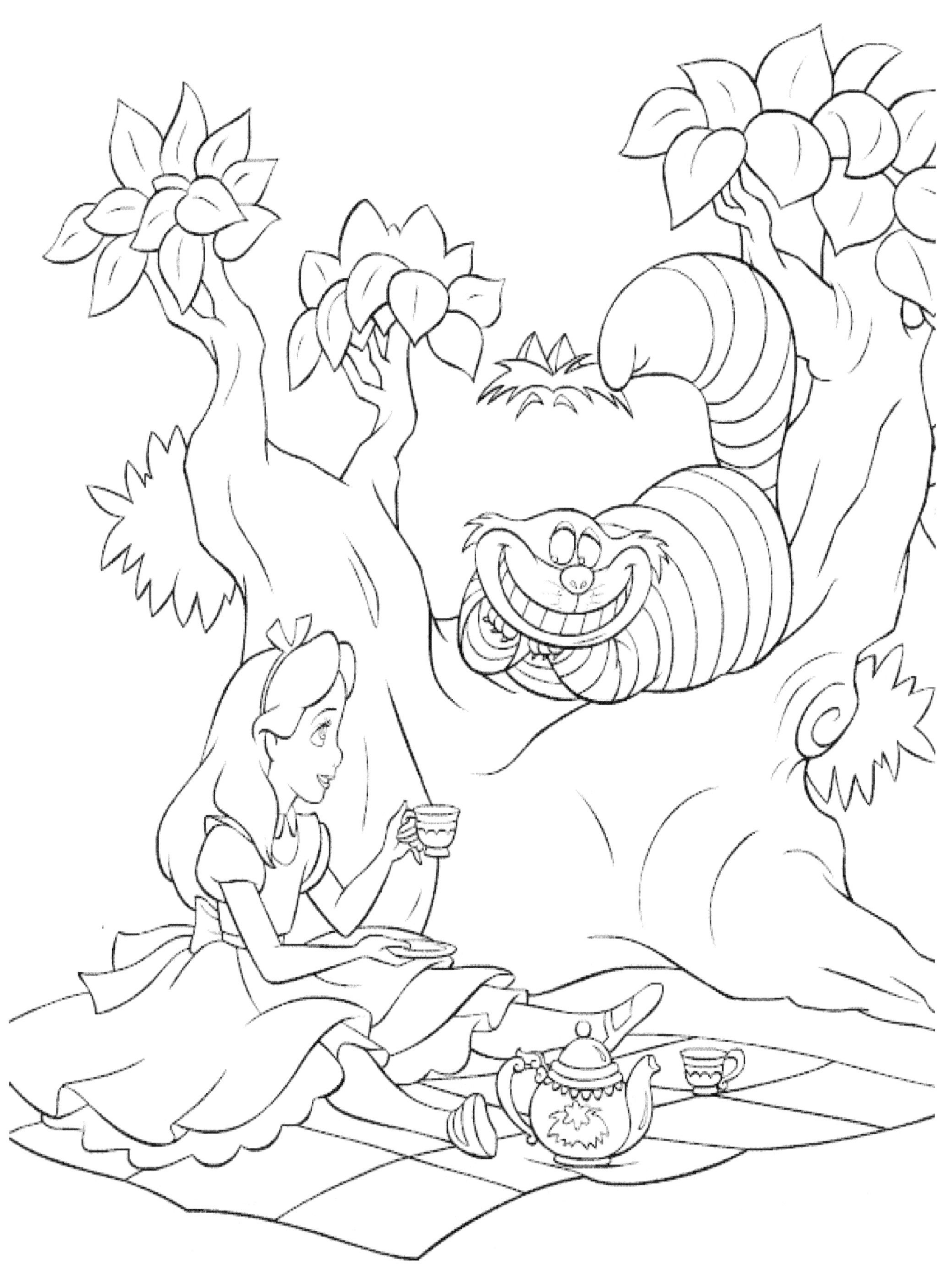

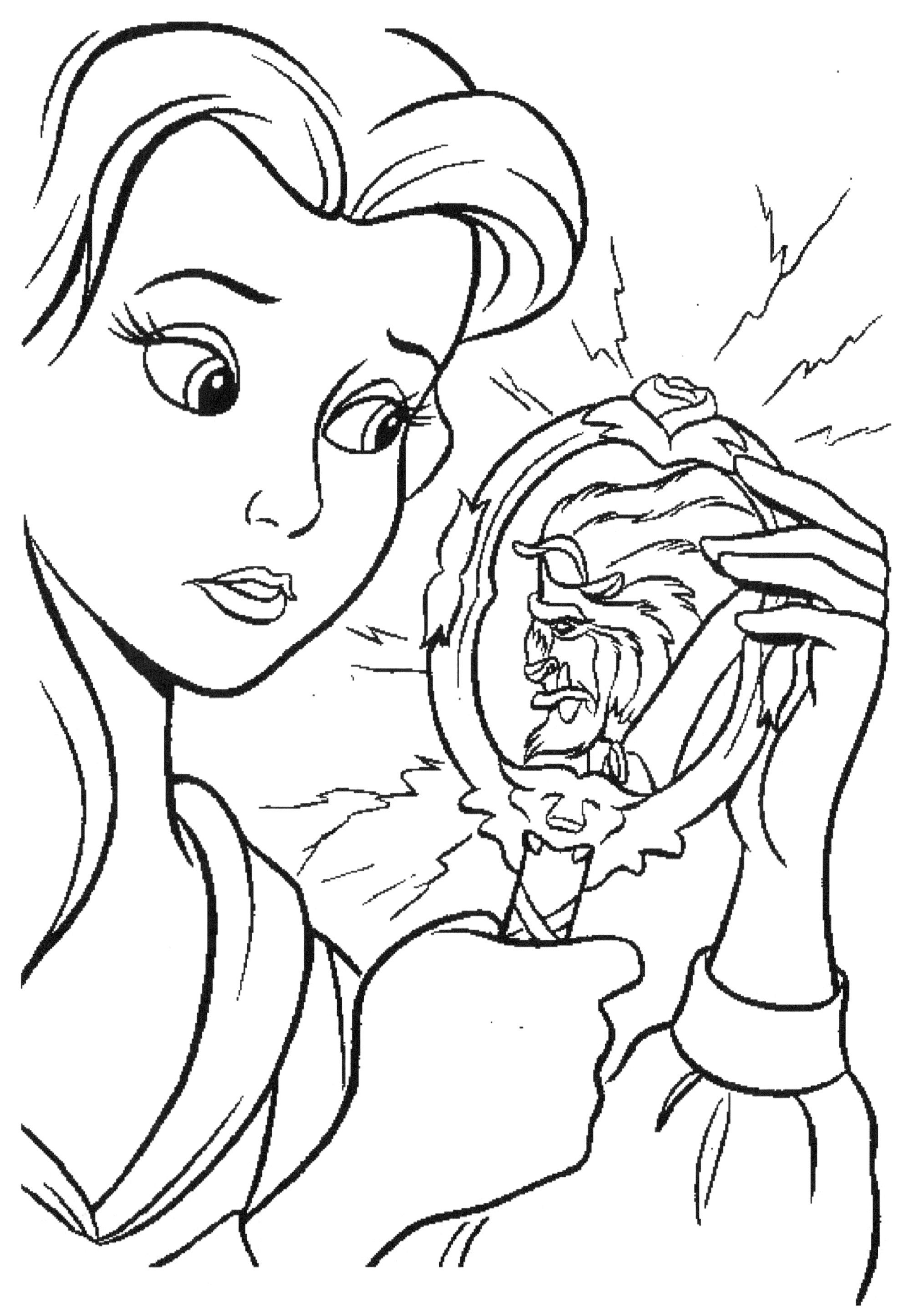

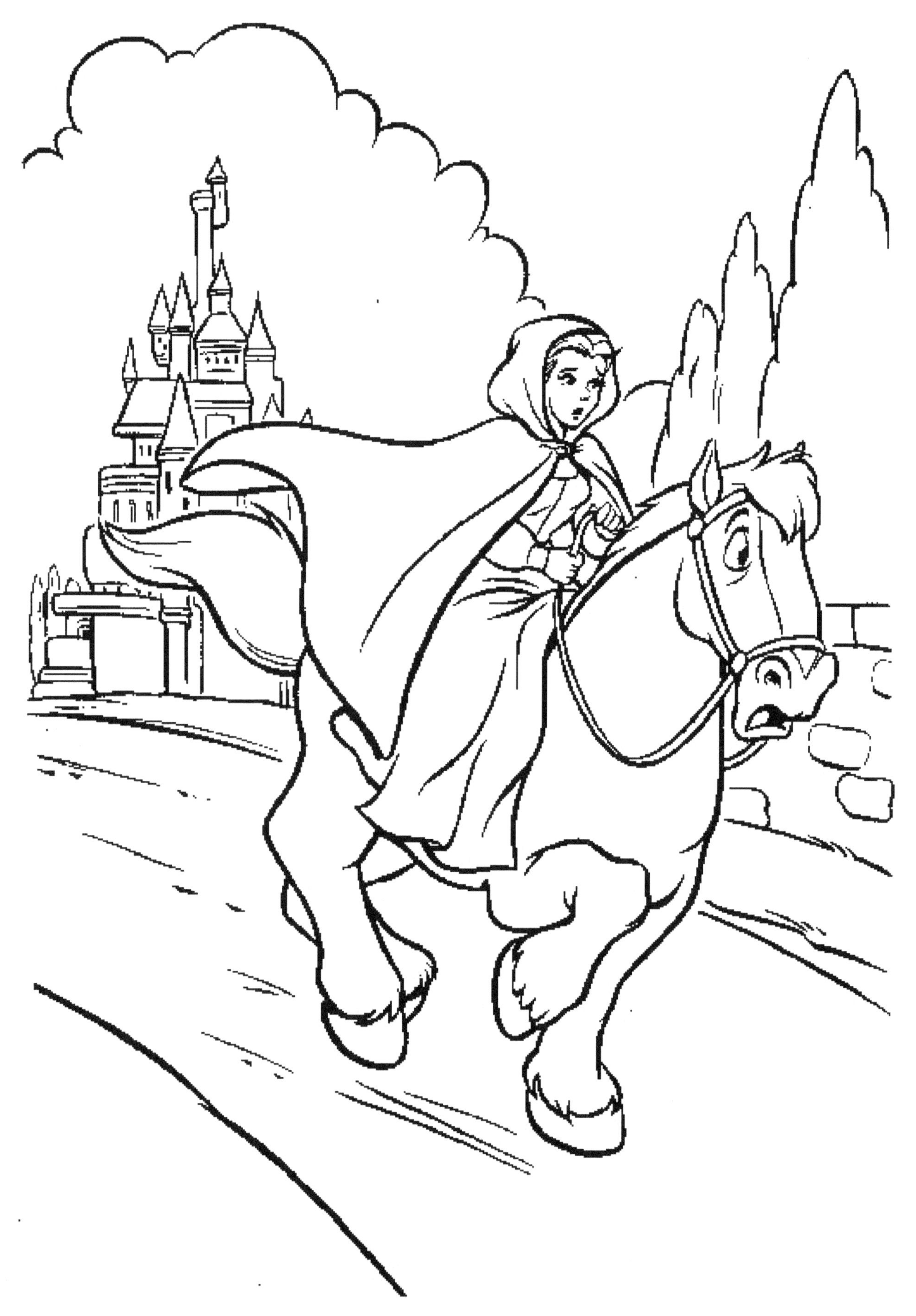

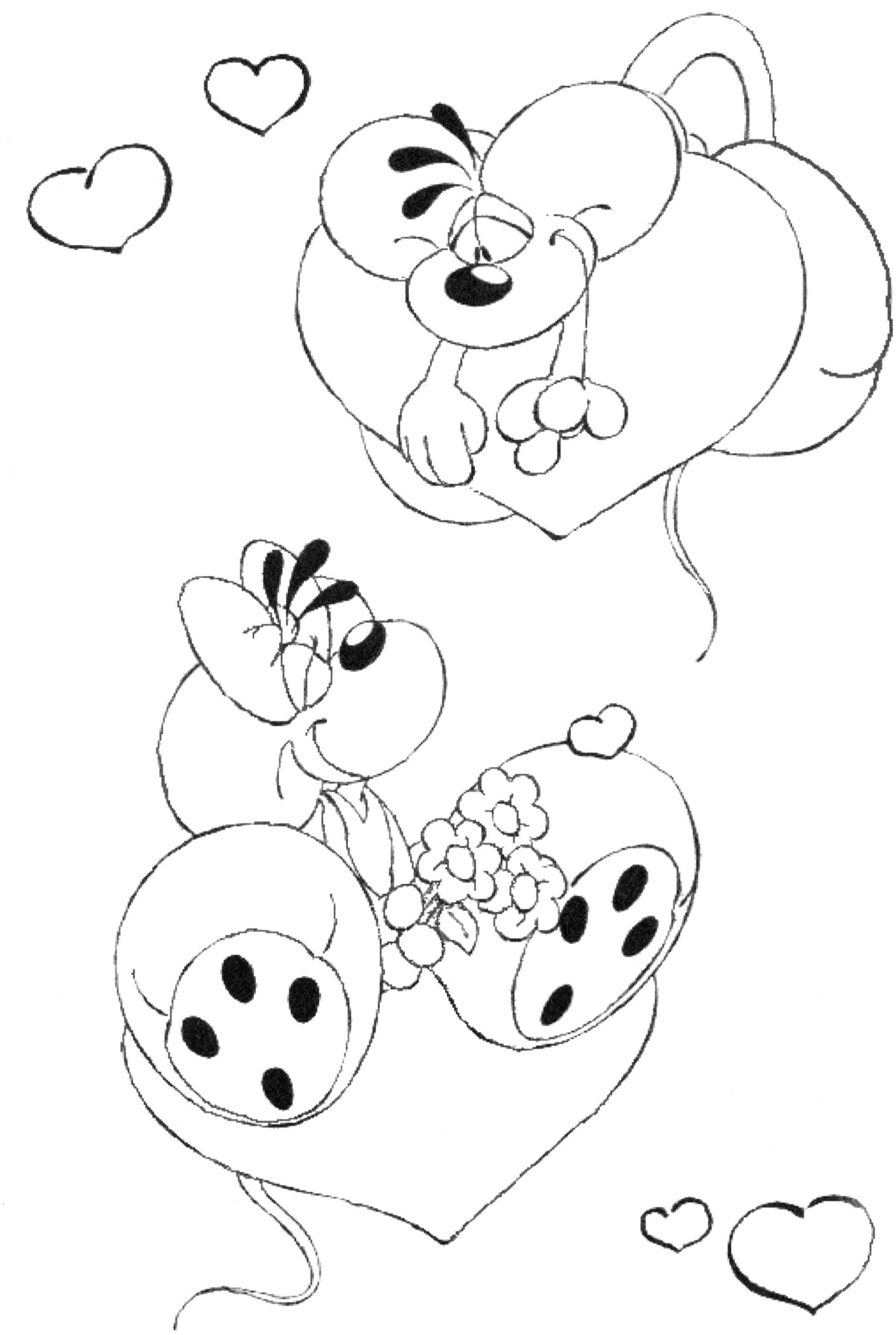

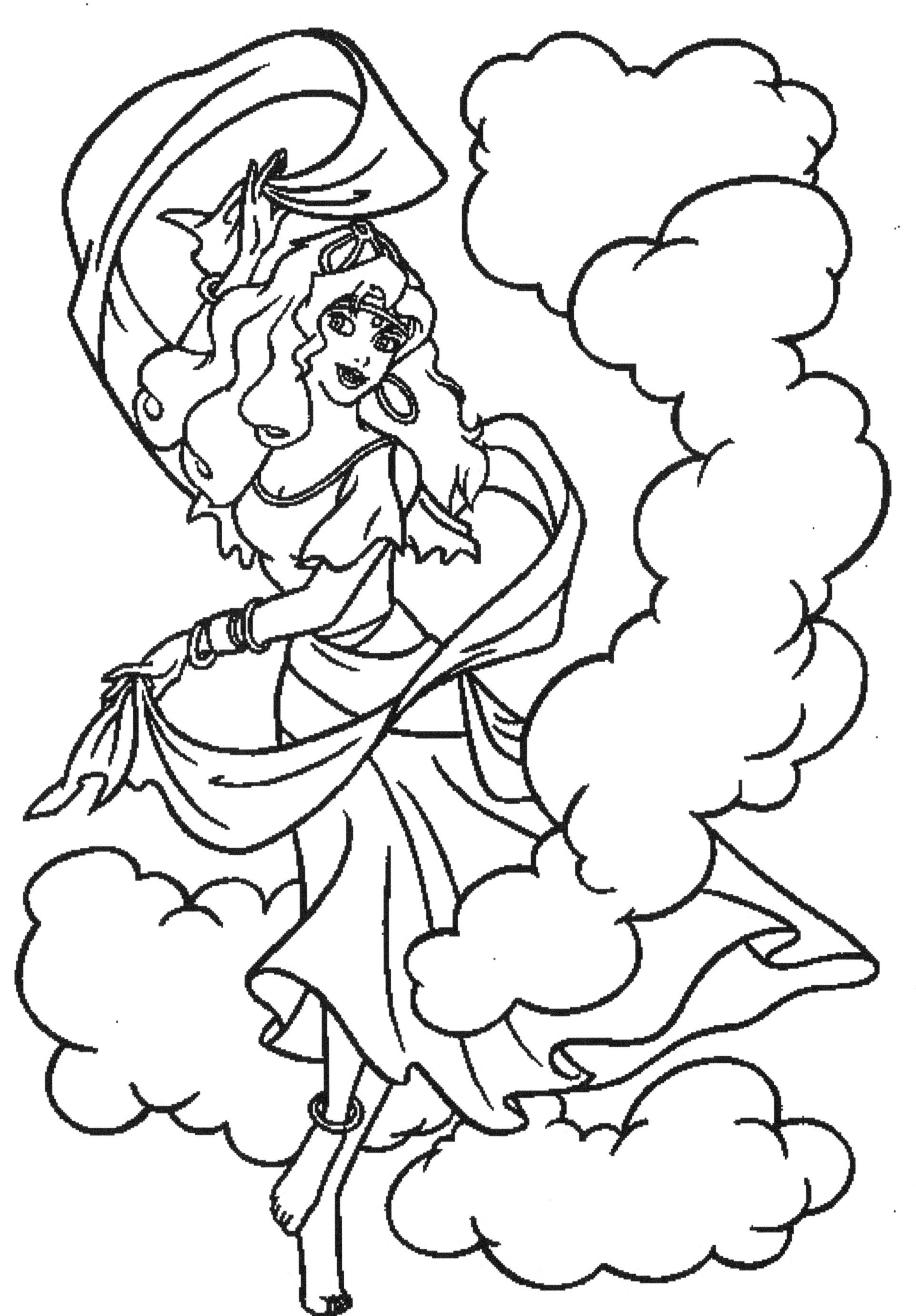

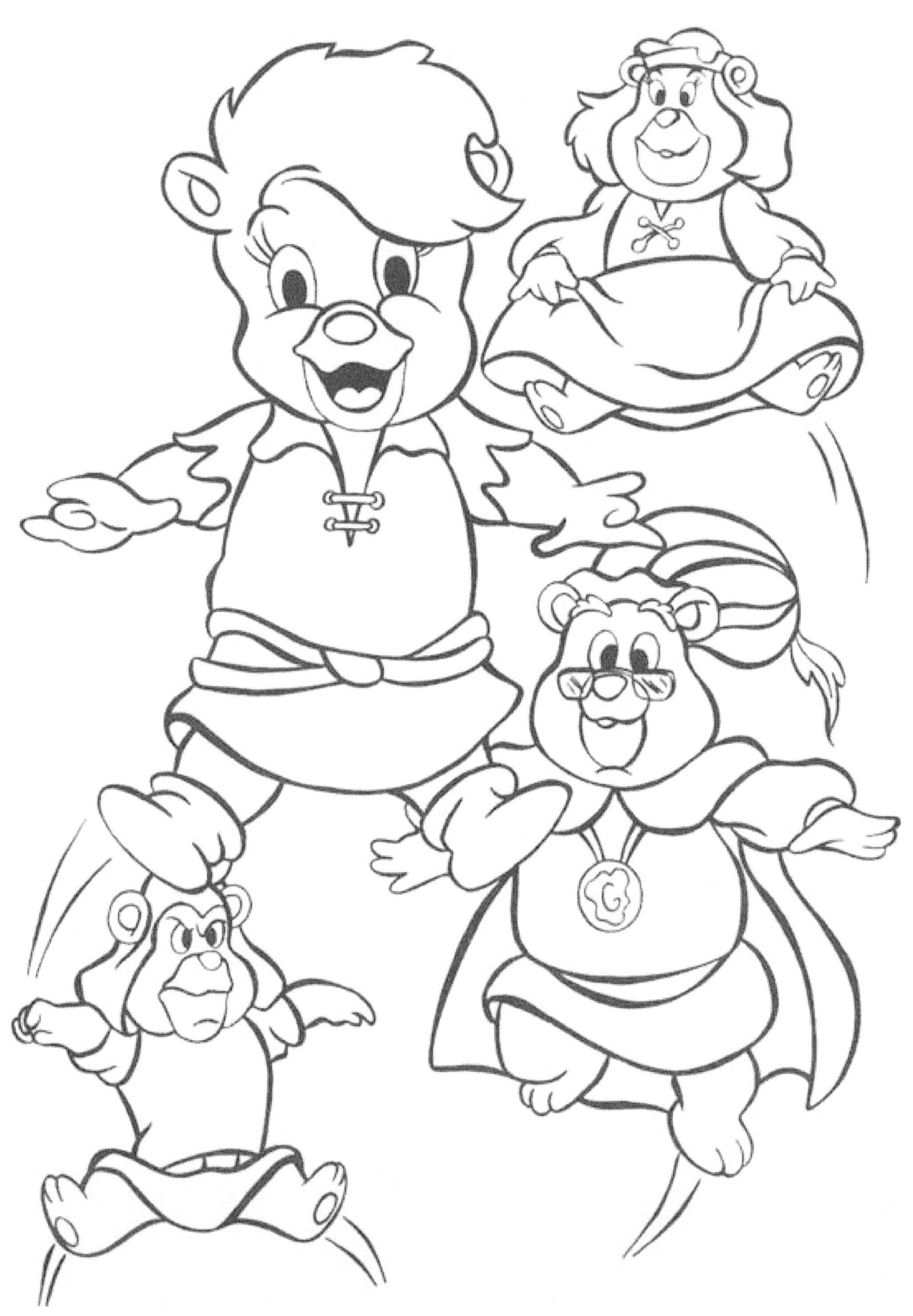

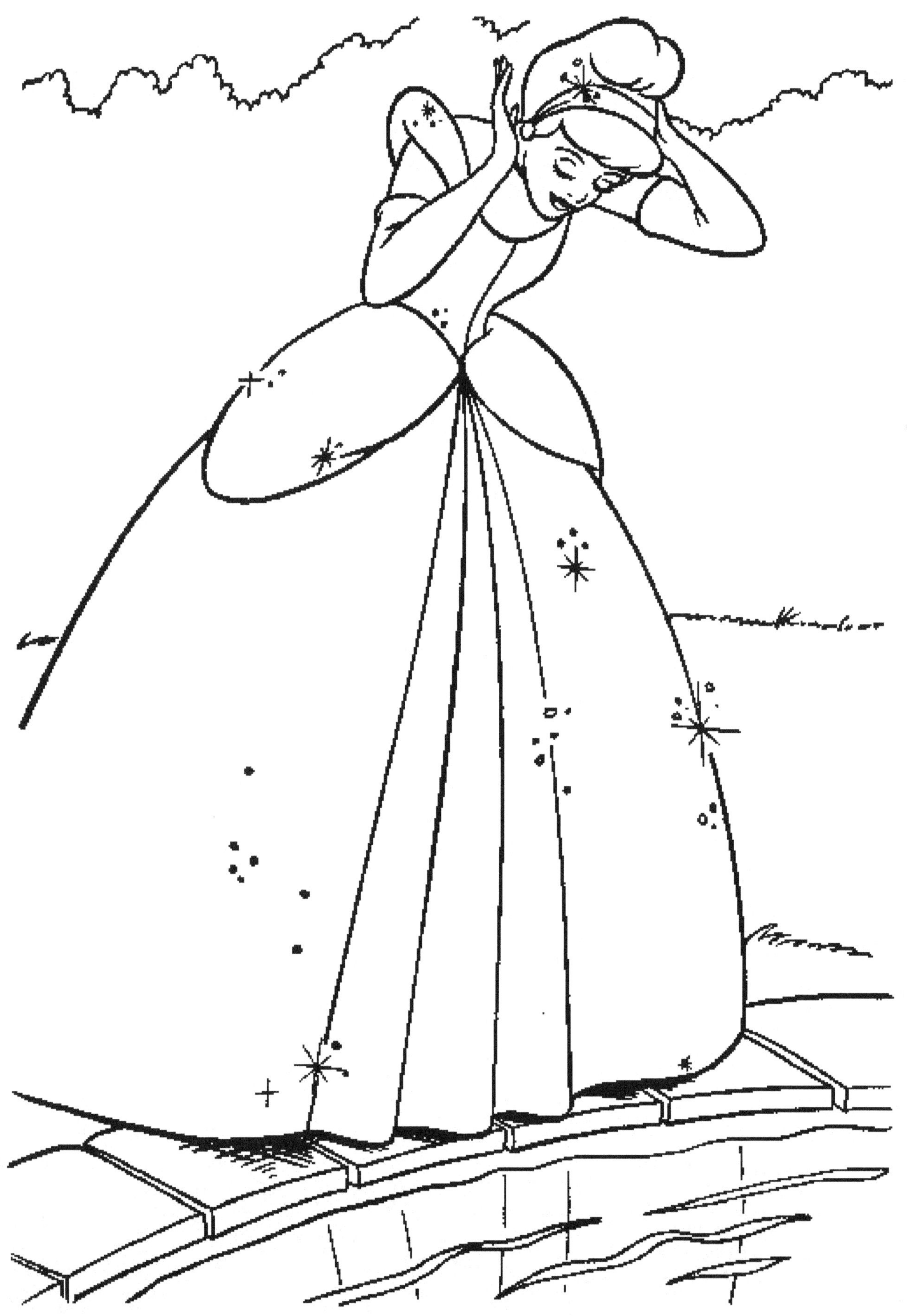

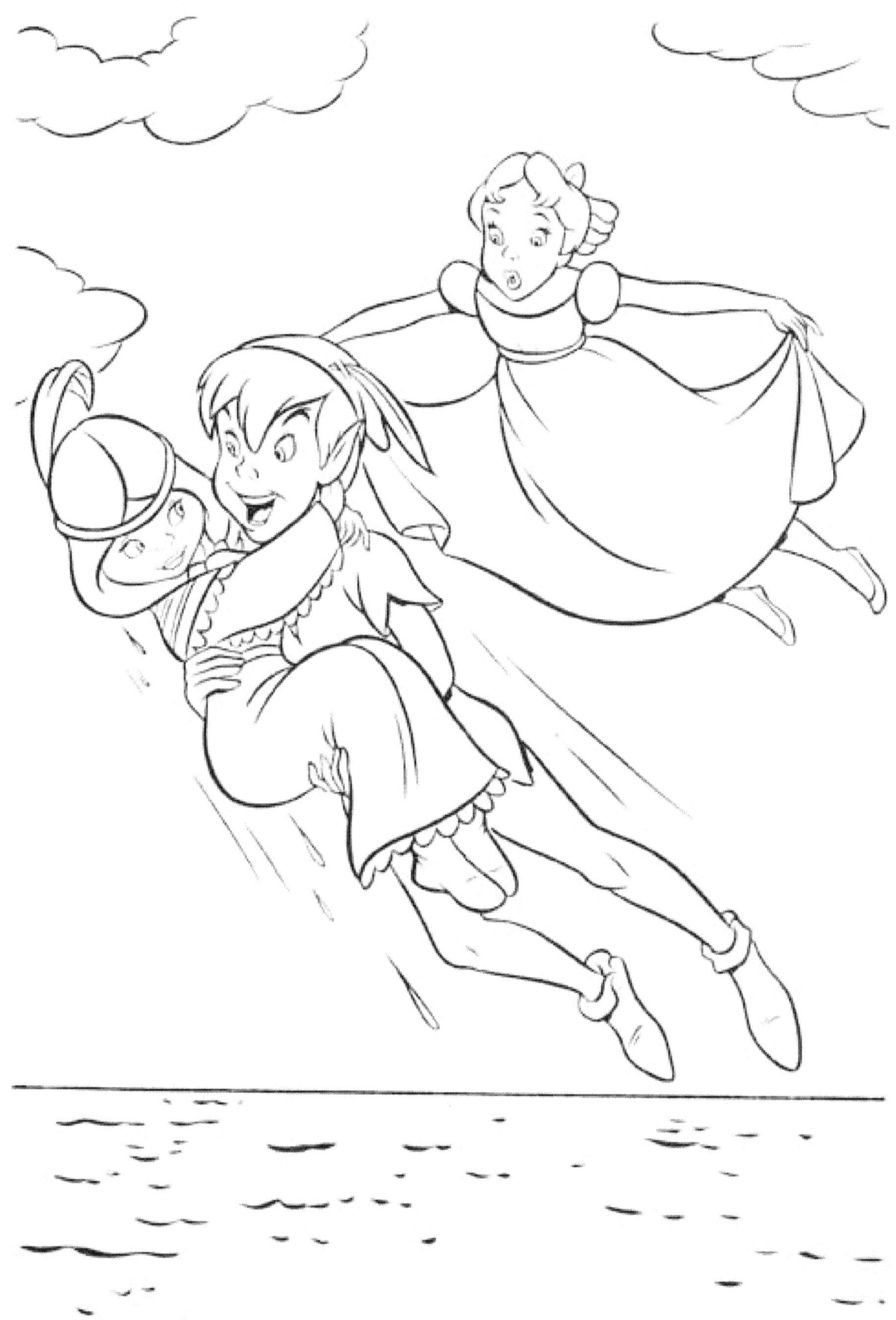

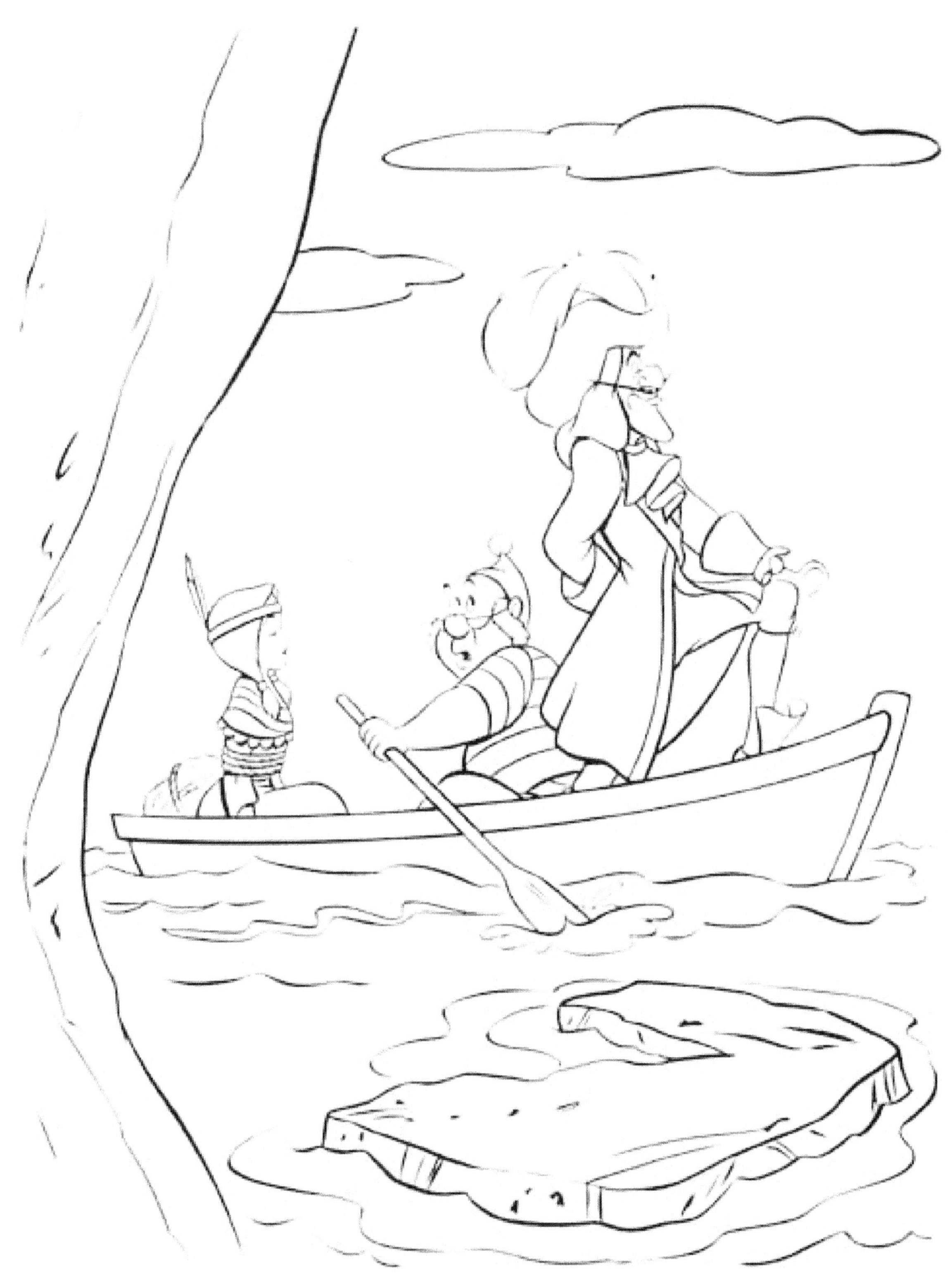

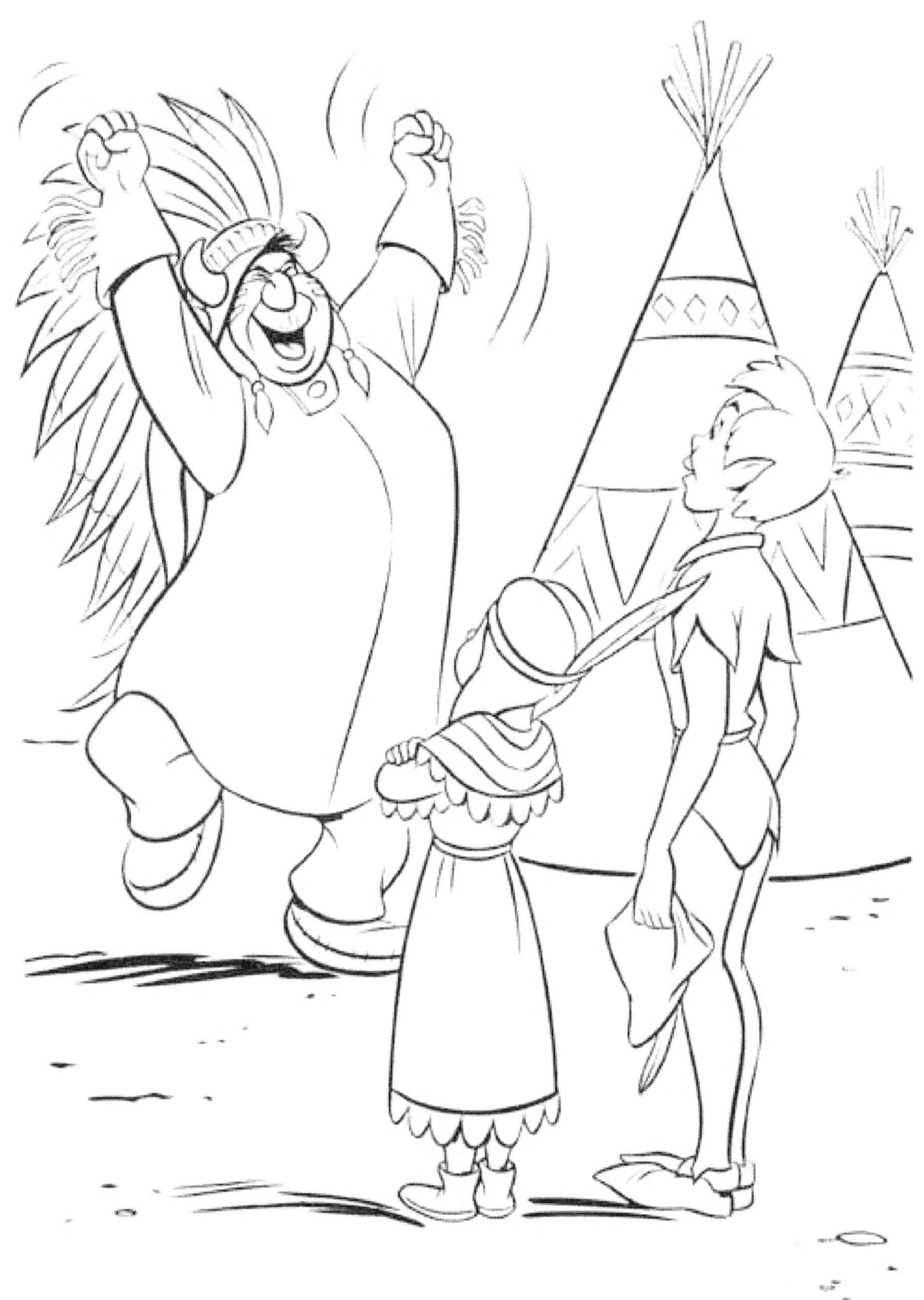

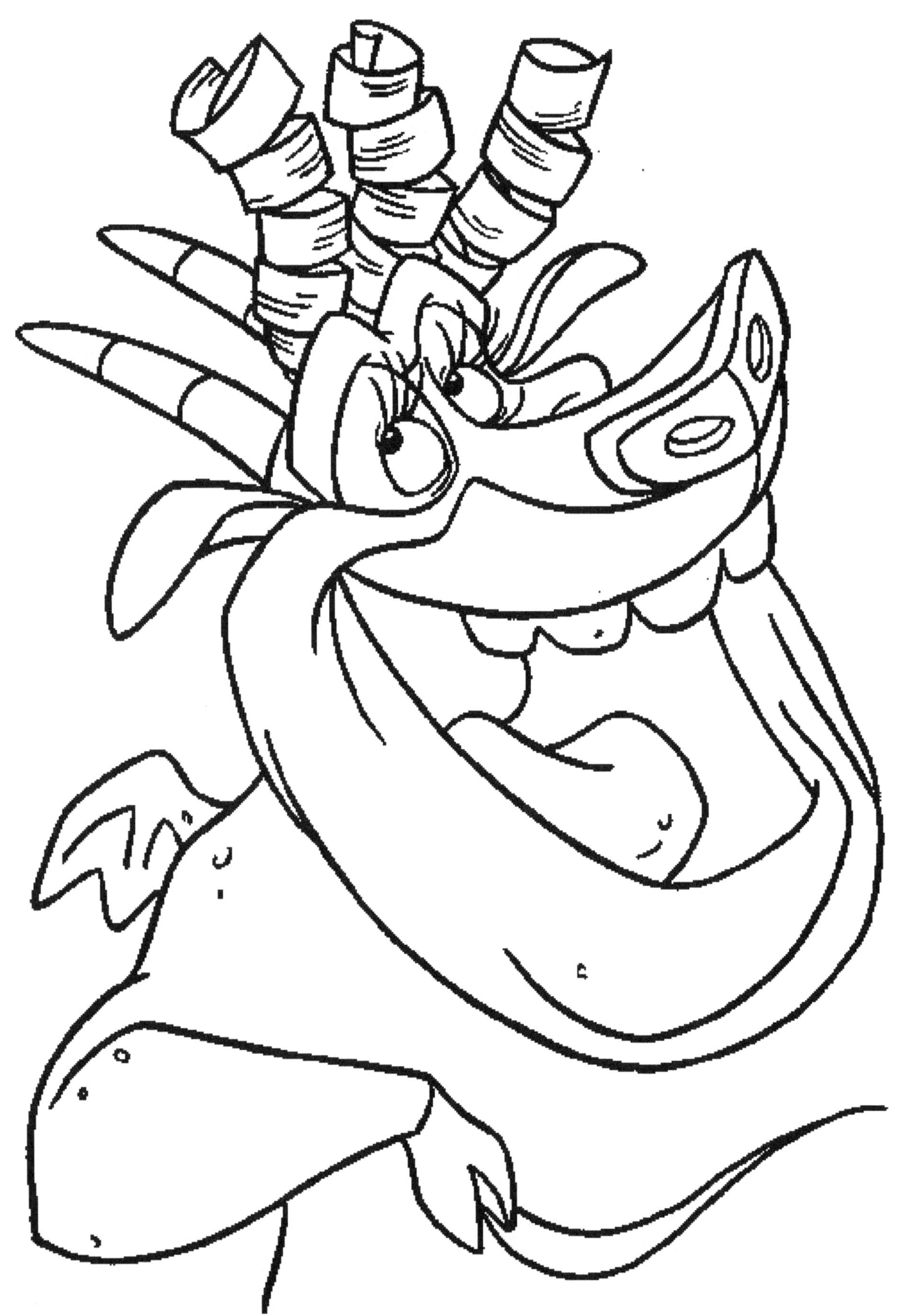

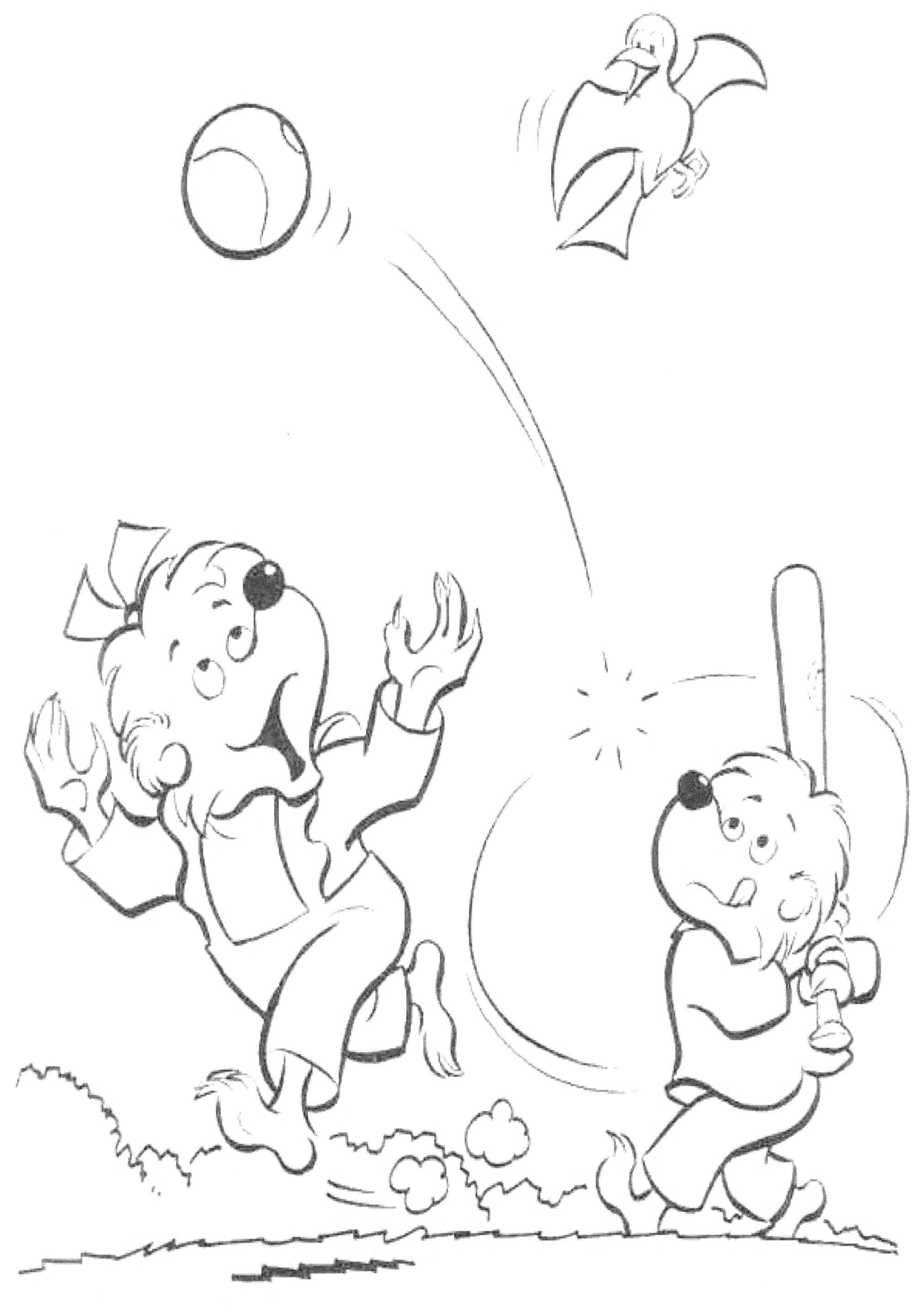

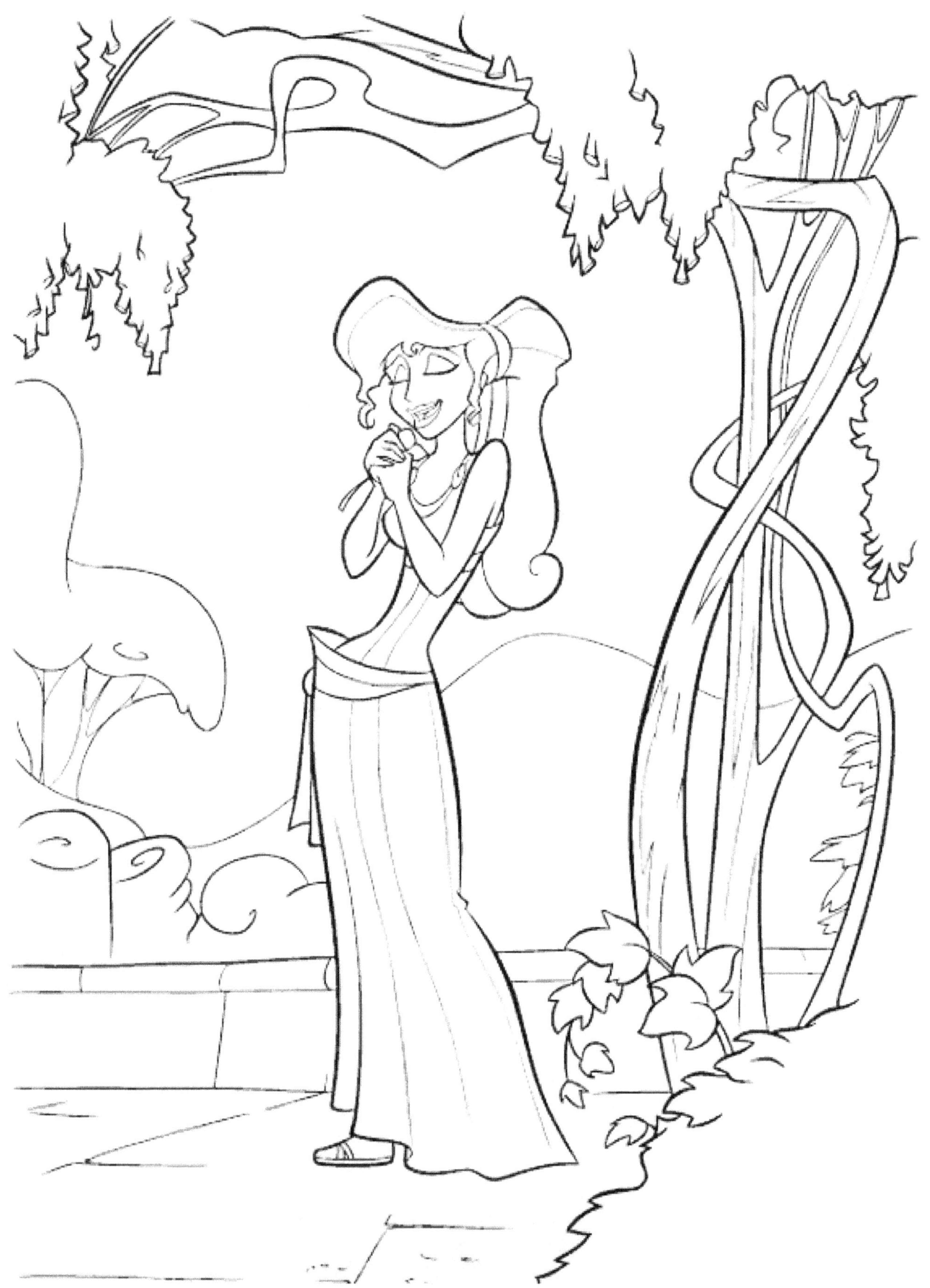

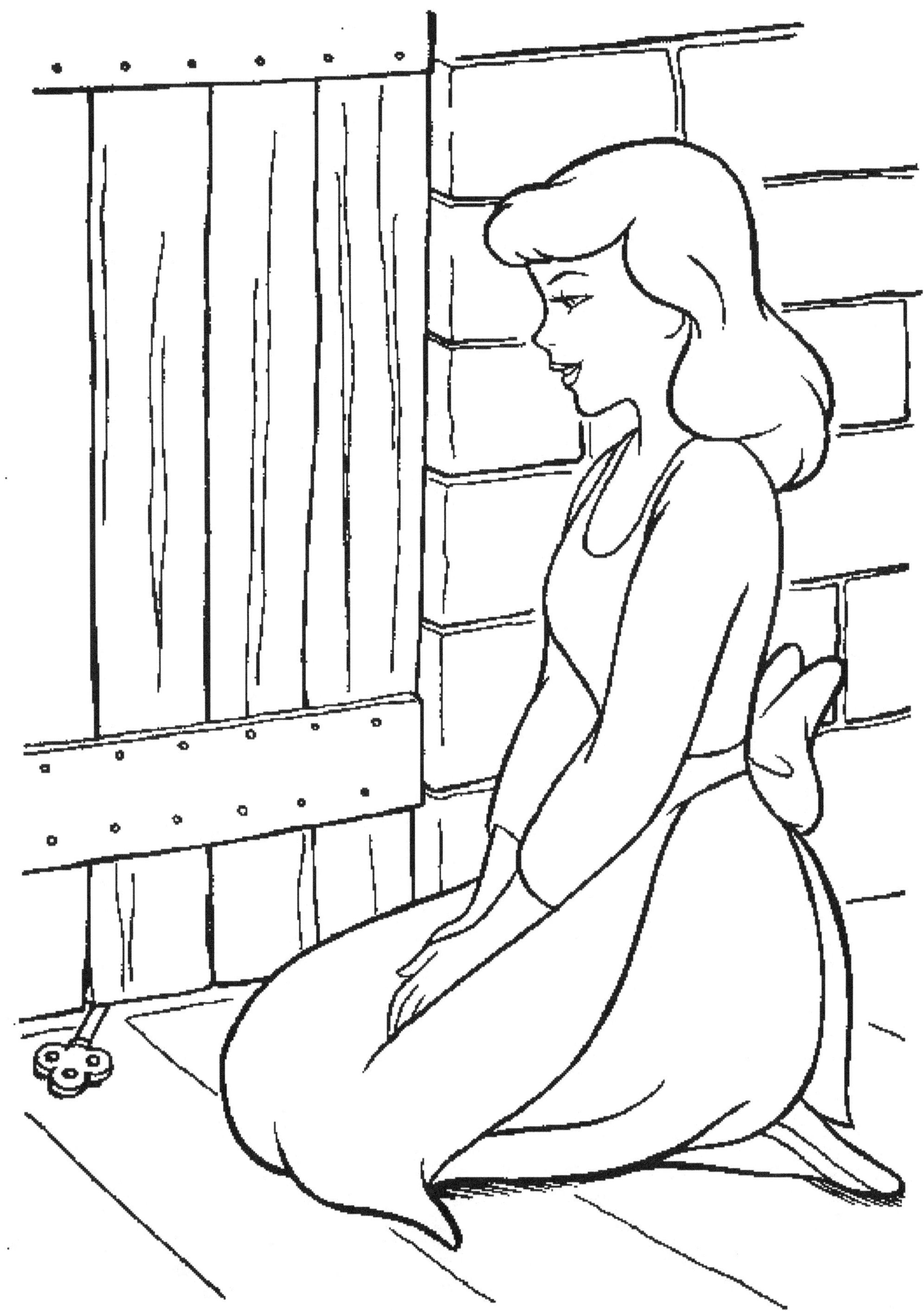

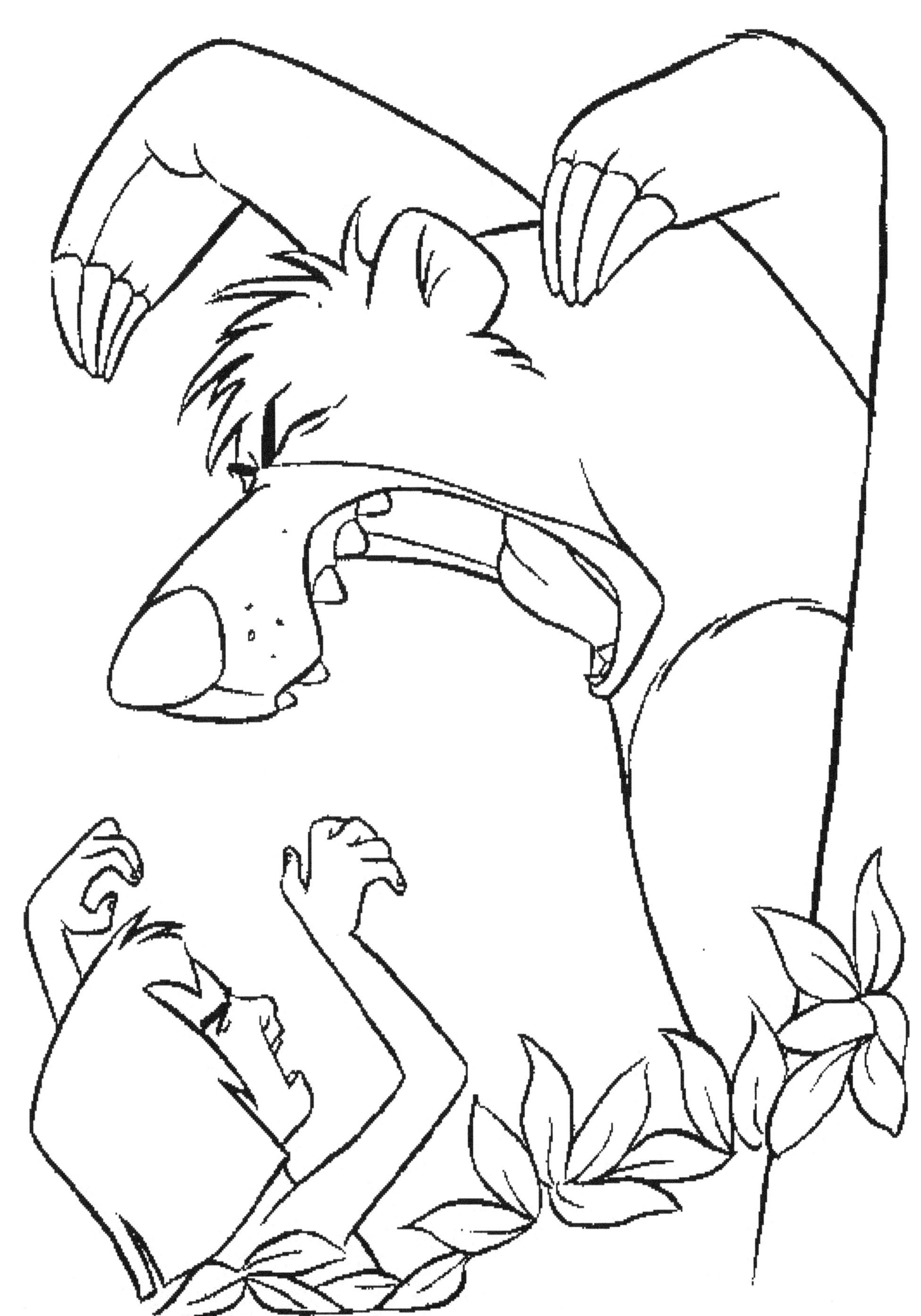

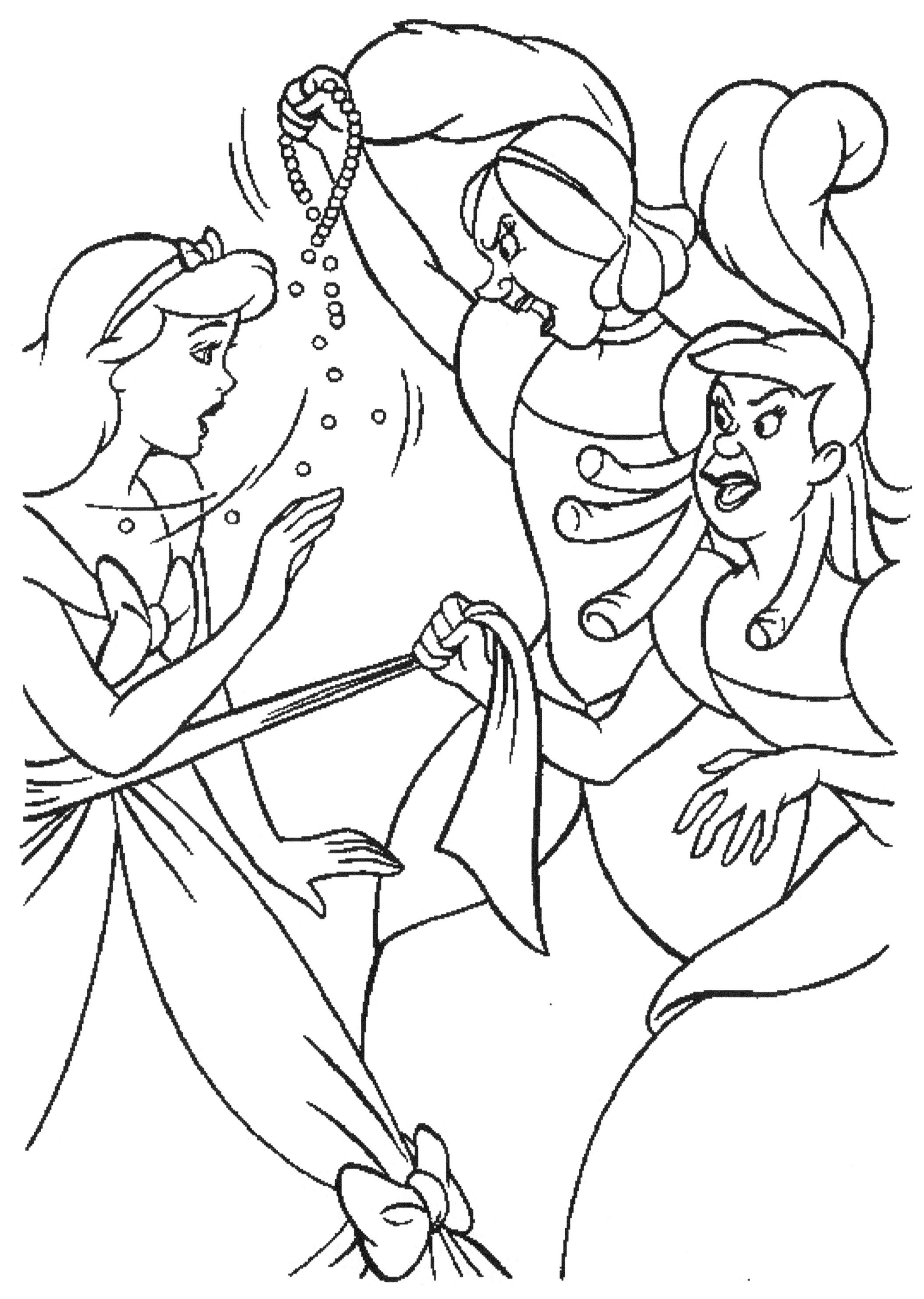

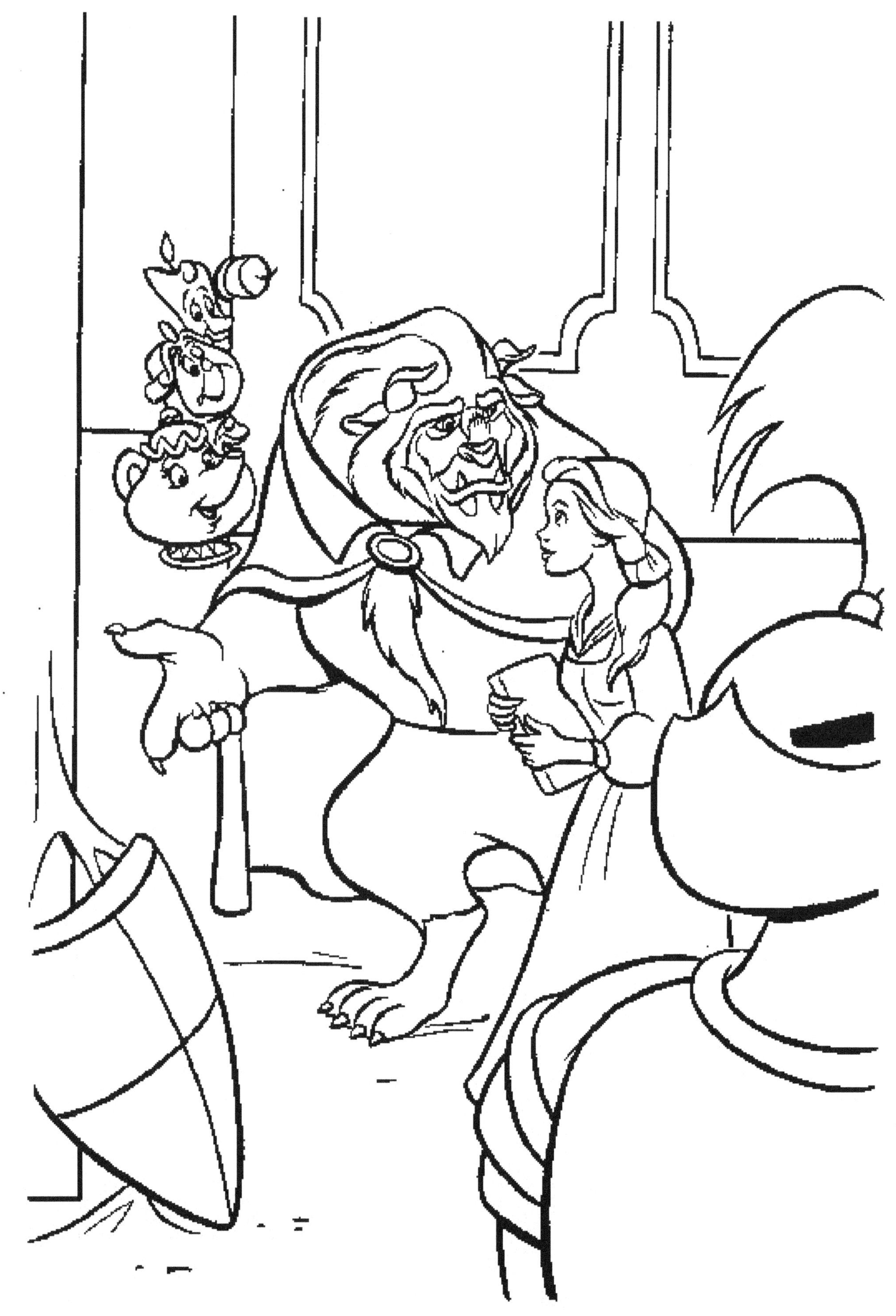

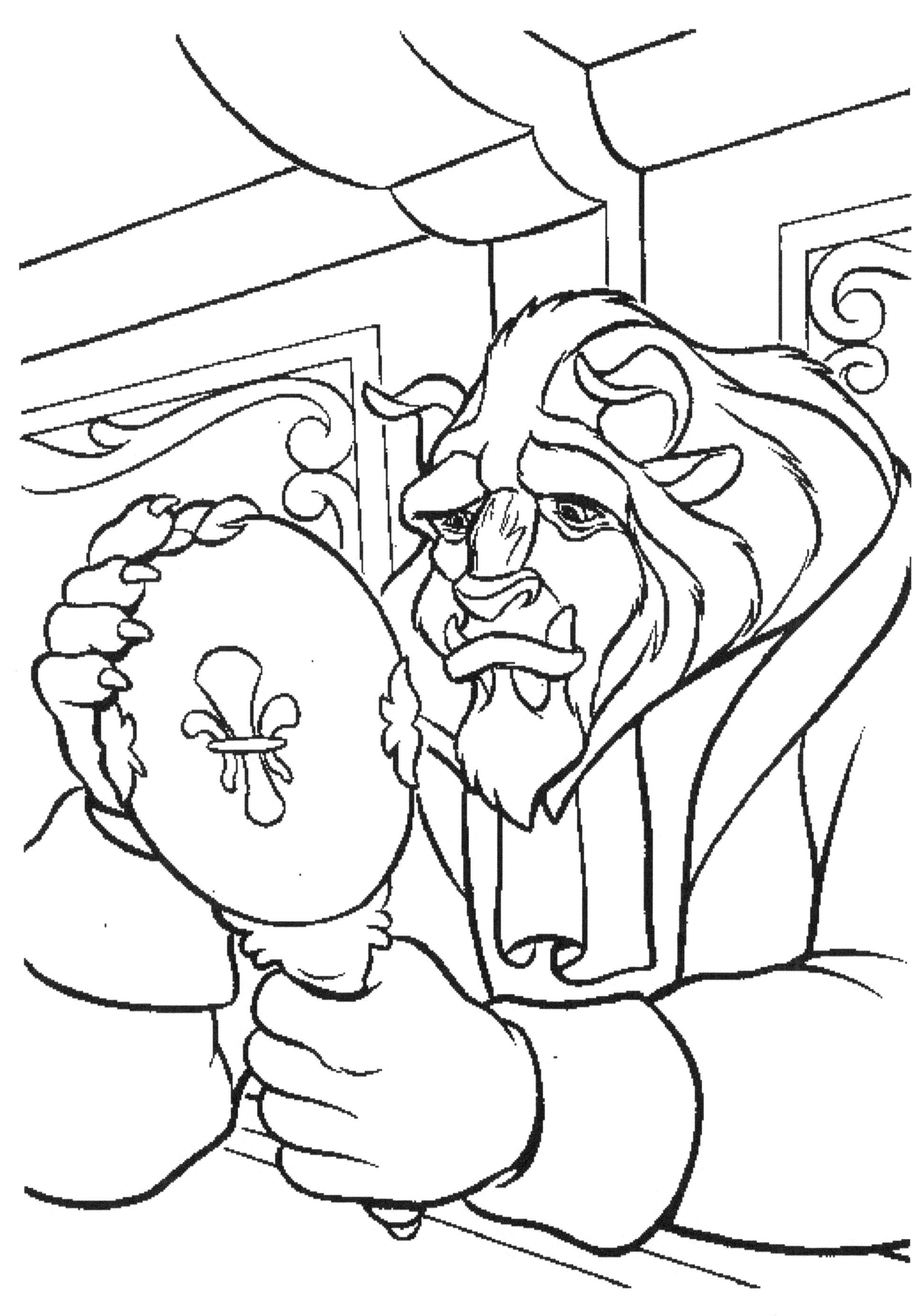

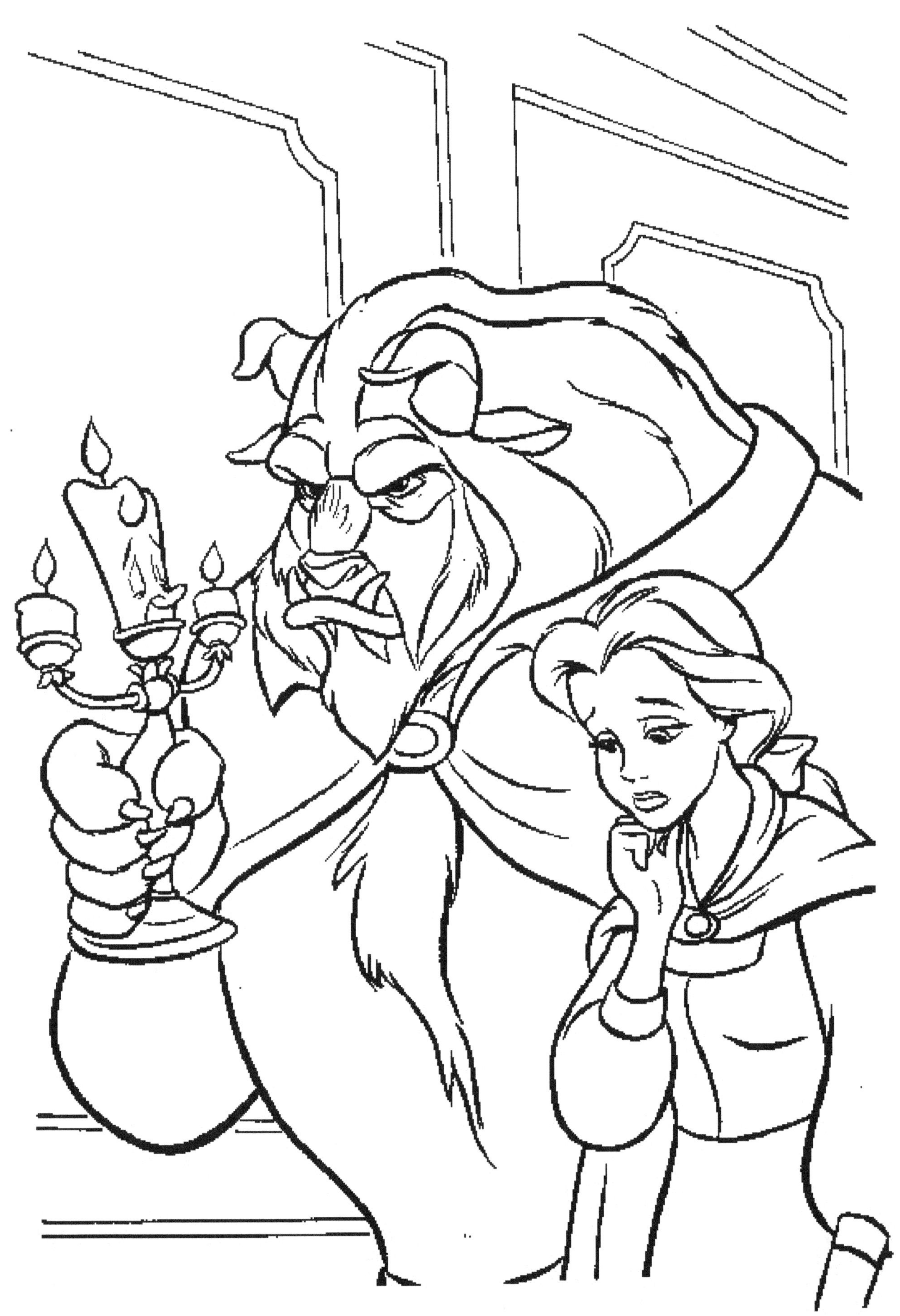

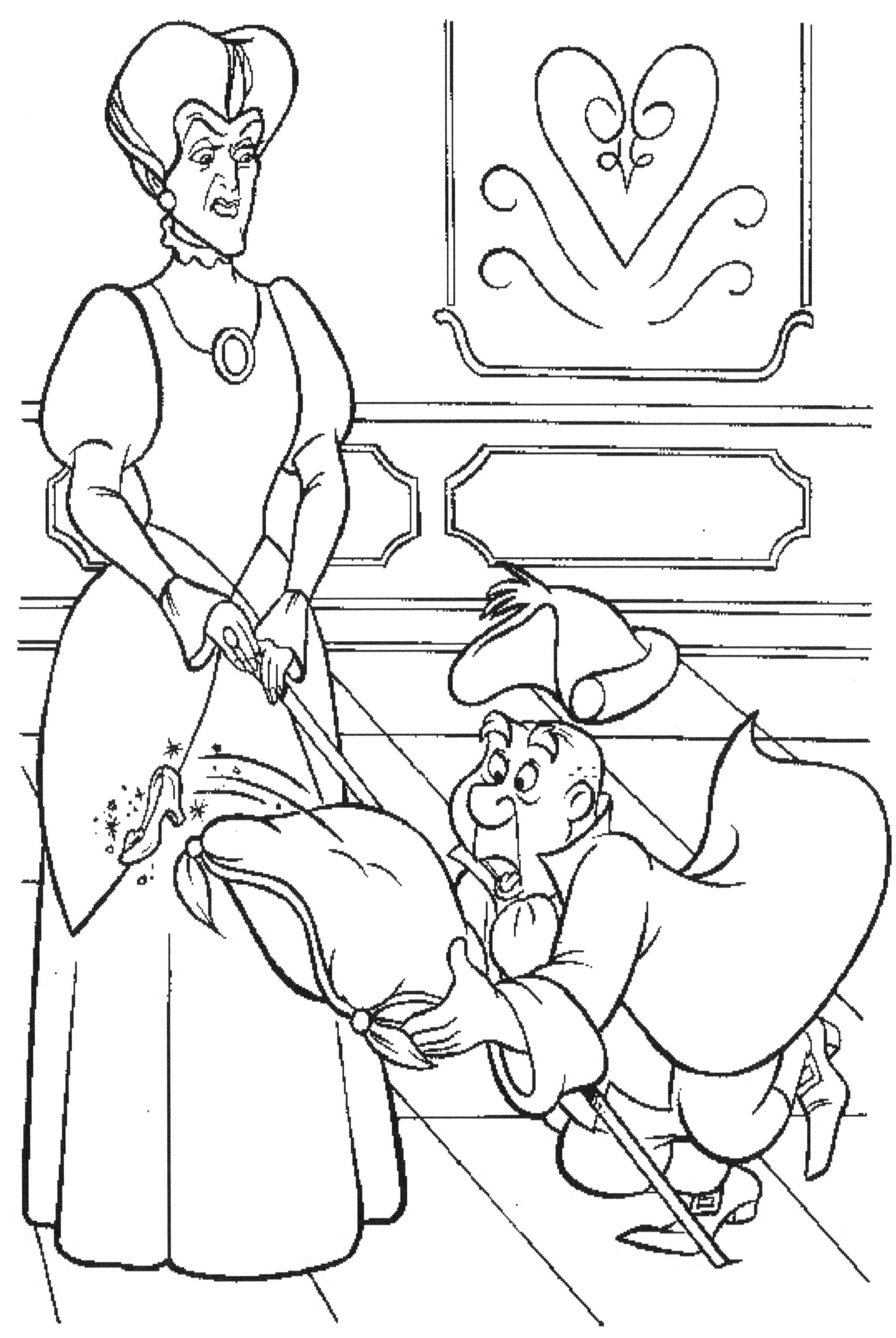

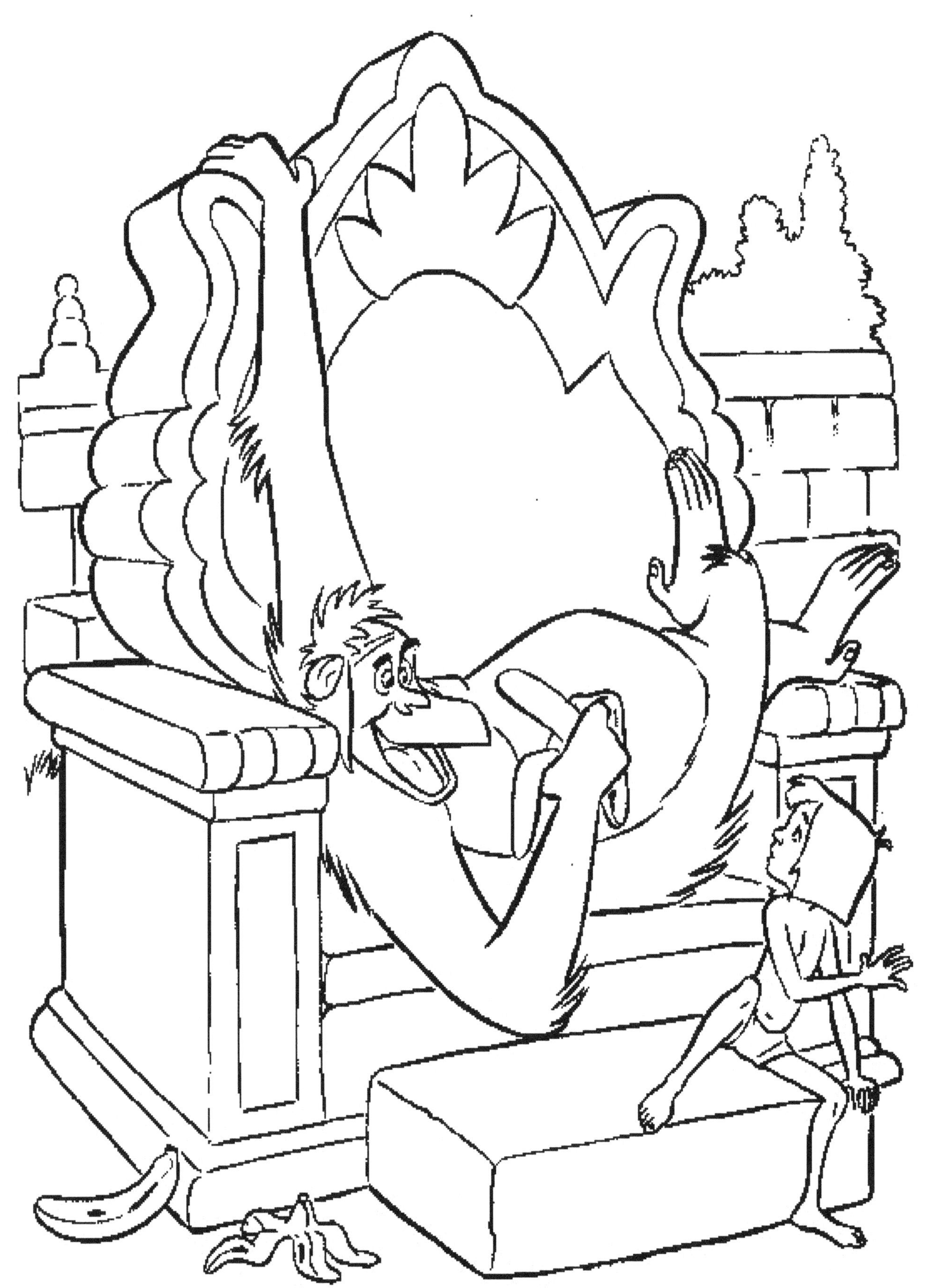

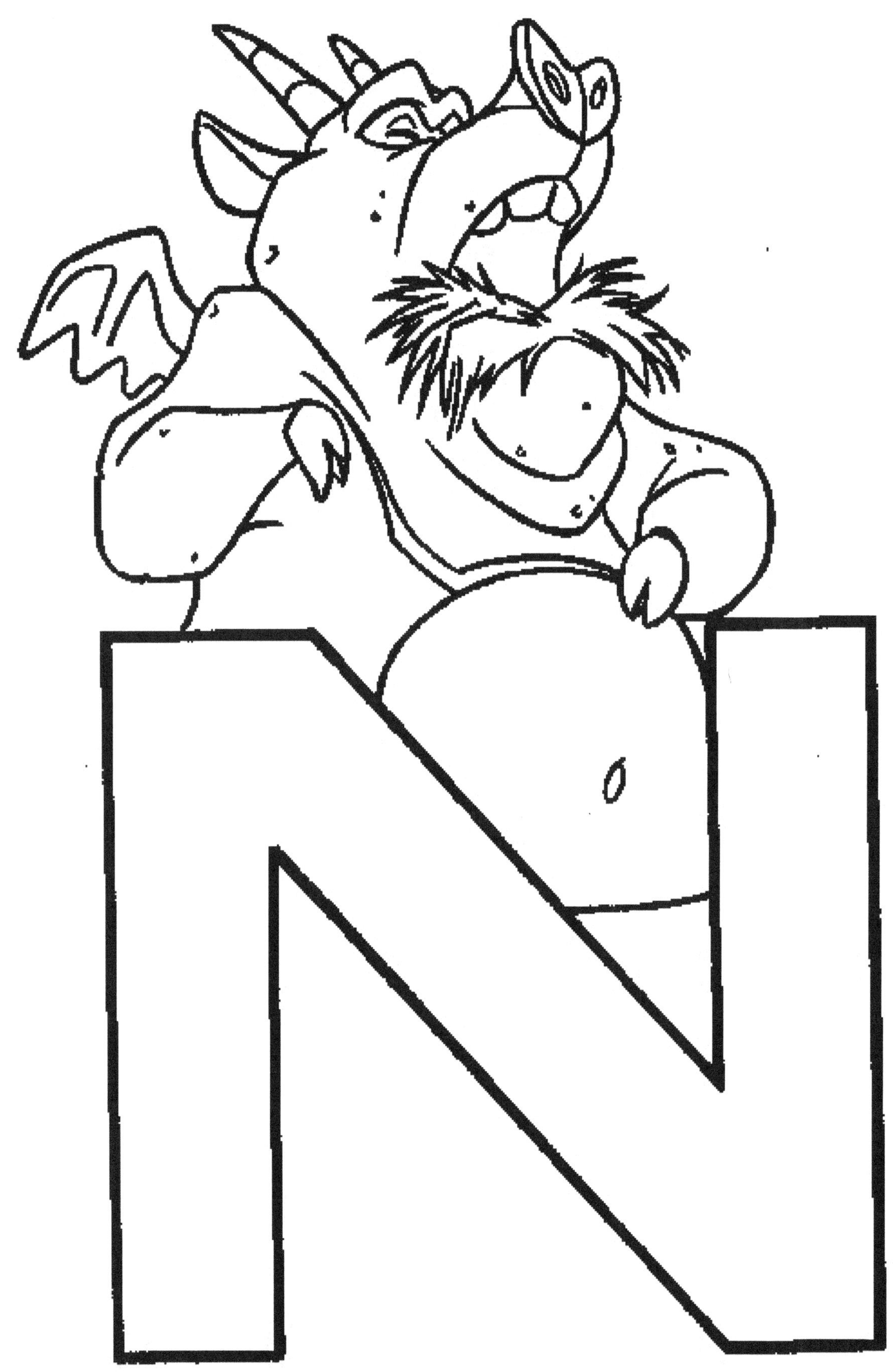

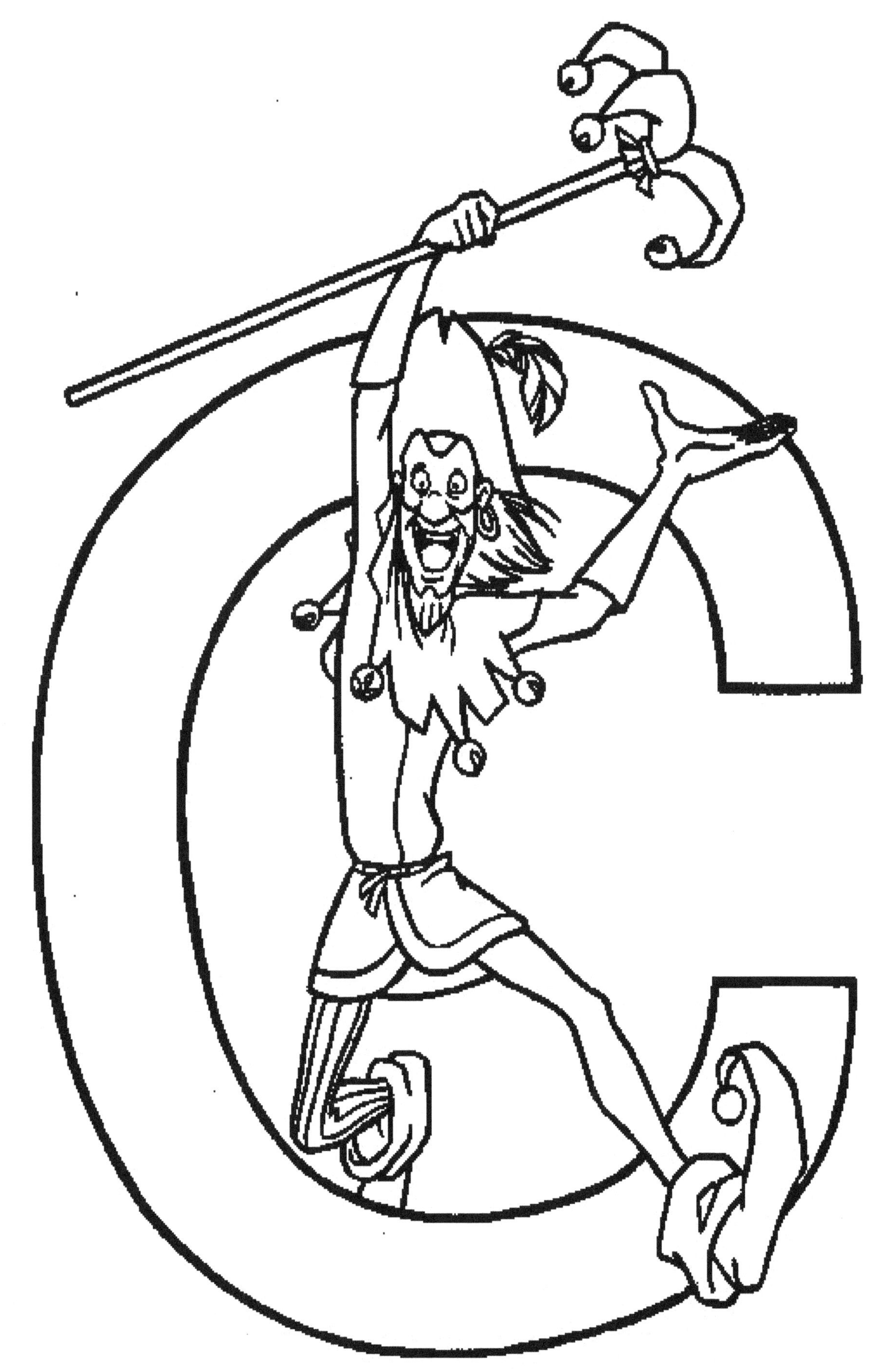

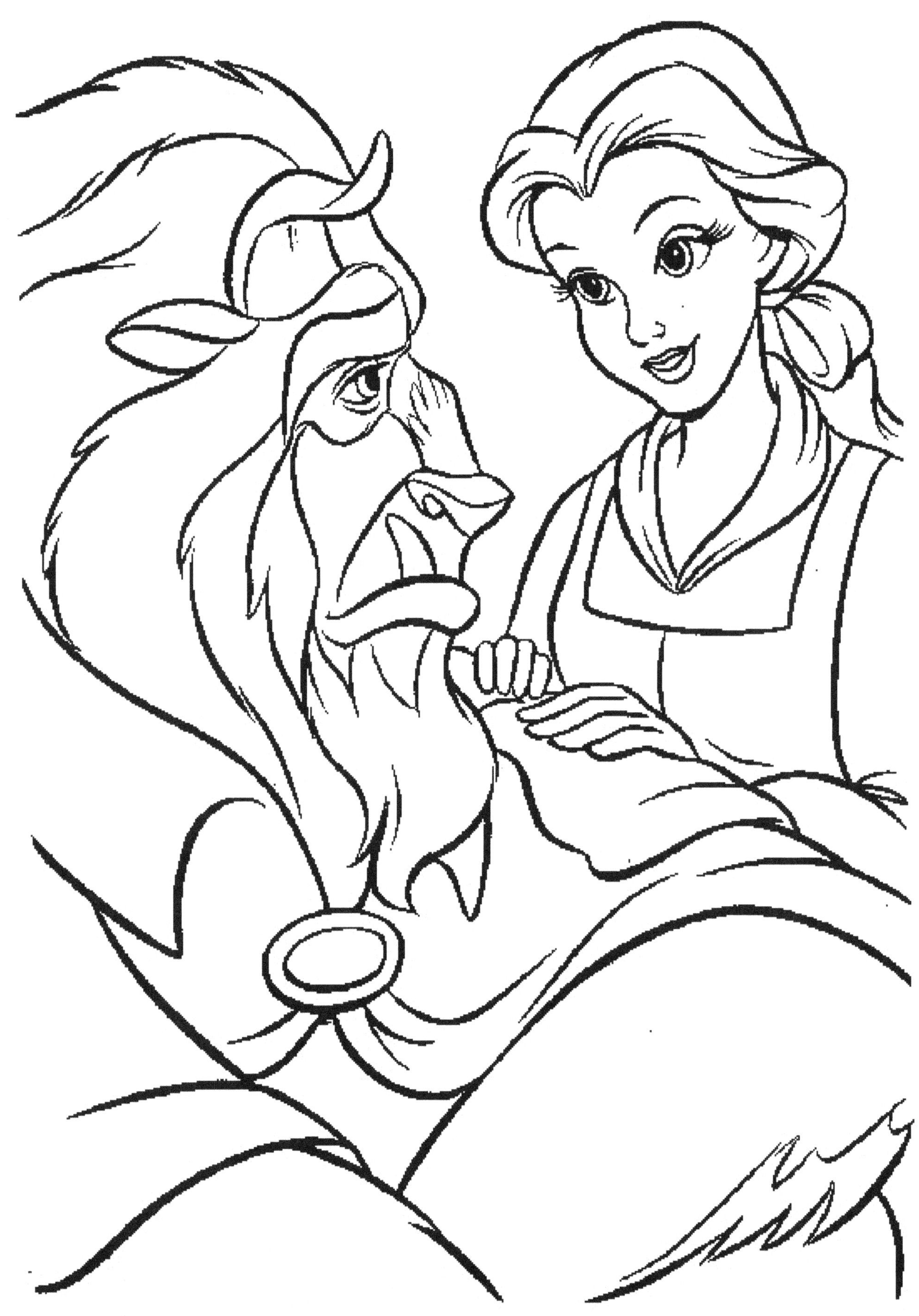

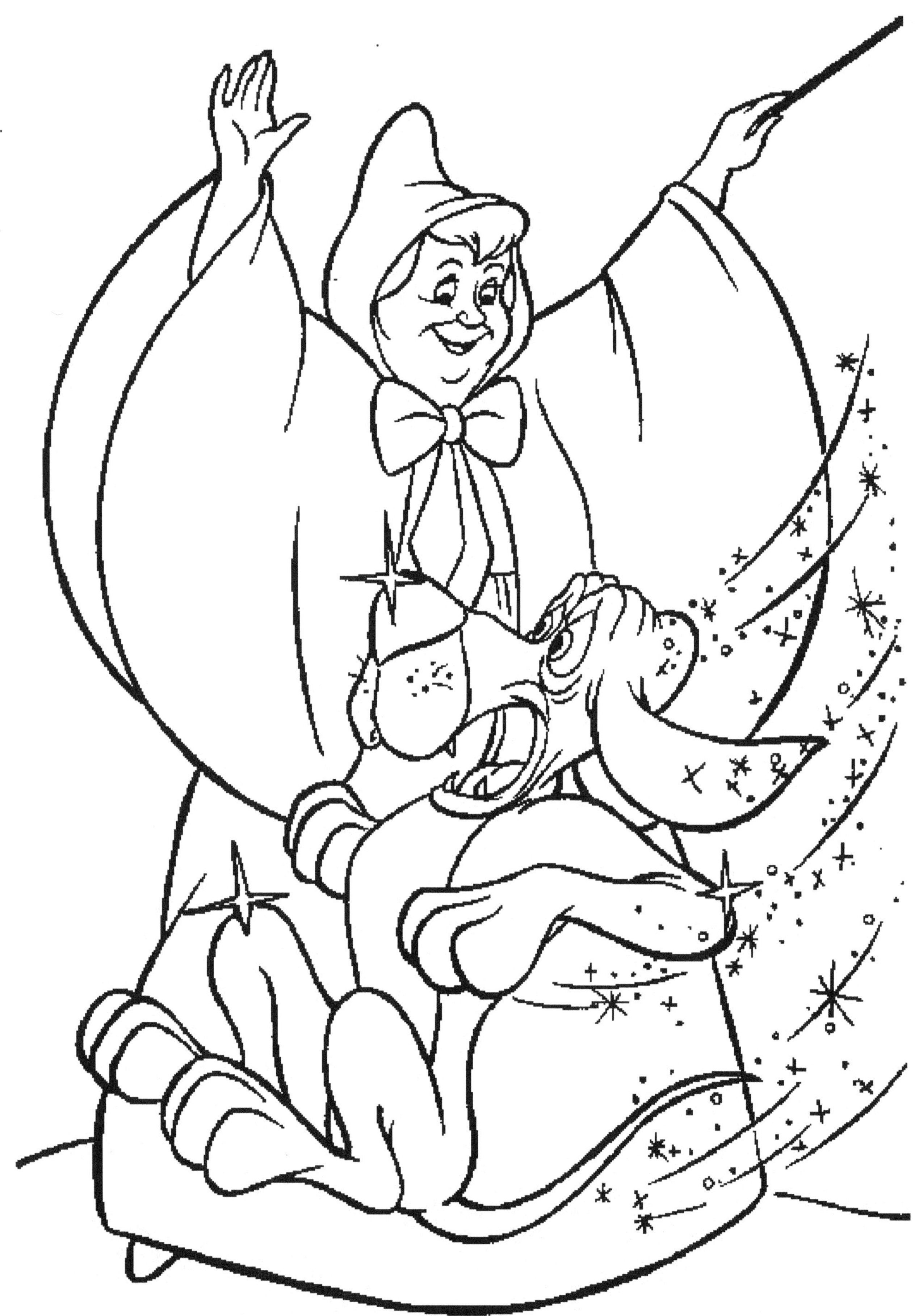

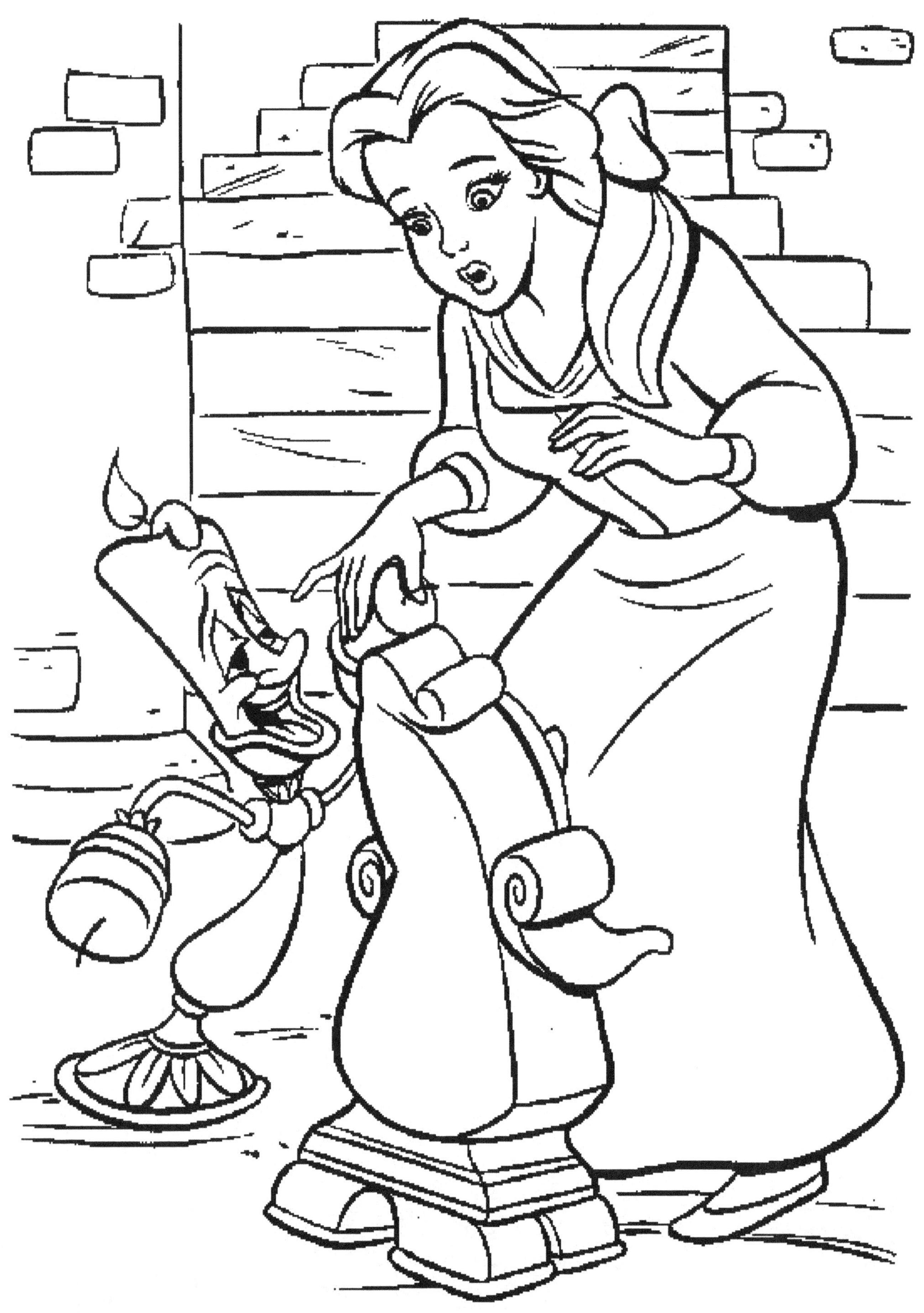

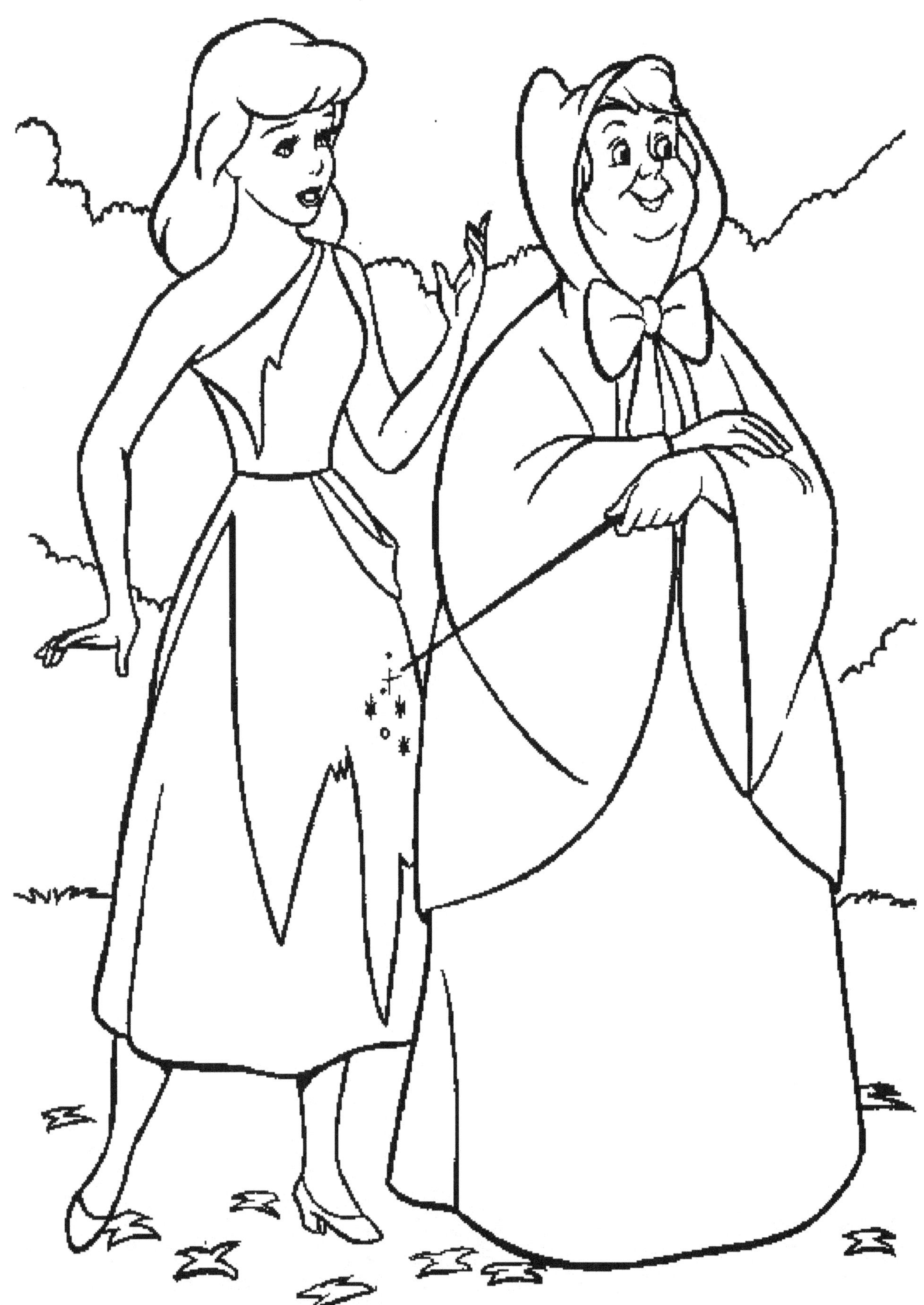

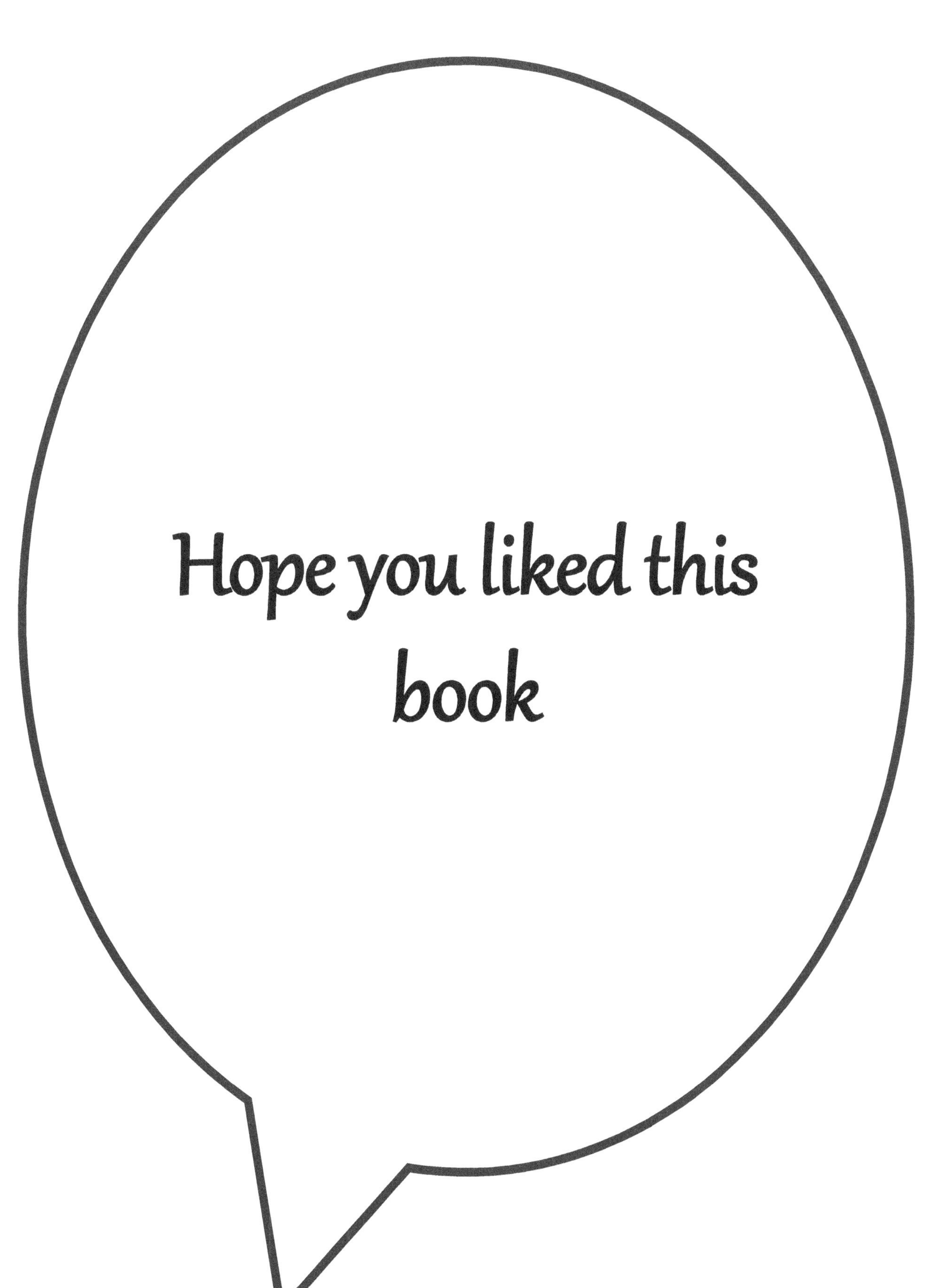

Hope you liked this
book

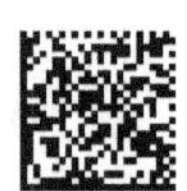

www.ingramcontent.com/pod-product-compliance
Lightning Source LLC
Chambersburg PA
CBHW081404130726
47998CB00011B/3065